# The "Genesis Controversy" and Continuity in Southern Baptist Chaos

## A Eulogy for a Great Tradition

D1291943

# The "Genesis Controversy"

and Continuity in Southern Baptist
Chaos • A Eulogy for a Great Tradition

## Ralph H. Elliott

Mercer University Press
Macon, Georgia

ISBN 0-86554-415-8                                    MUP/P098

🍂🍂🍂

🍂🍂🍂

*Library of Congress Cataloging-in-Publication Data*
Elliott, Ralph H.
The "Genesis controversy"and continuity in Southern Baptist chaos.
A eulogy for a great tradition. / by Ralph H. Elliott.
xvi+178 pages. 6x9" (15x23 cm.).
Includes bibliographical references.
ISBN 0-86554-415-8 (alk. paper).
1. Elliott, Ralph H.
2. Elliott, Ralph H. The message of Genesis.
3. Southern Baptist Convention—History.
4. Midwestern Baptist Theological Seminary (U.S.).
5. Old Testament scholars—United States—Dismissal of. I. Title.
BX6495.E44A3          1992
286'.132—dc20          92-8645
CIP

# Contents

*Dedicated*
*to the women in my life*

**Virginia,**
**Virginia Lee, Beverly Ann**

*loving and supportive*
*wife and daughters*
*always there . . . always understanding*

*and remembering Virginia's words*

*"If you go down there and sell your soul,*
*don't come home."*

# Foreword

While reading Ralph Elliott's *The "Genesis Controversy" and Continuity in Southern Baptist Chaos,* I was not surprised to learn that Elliott still expresses a kind, nonvindictive attitude toward those whose unjust attacks and unfair hearings ended his teaching career in Southern Baptist theological education. When I arrived on the new campus of Midwestern Baptist Theological Seminary in 1959, the attack was already rather fully developed. Throughout the turmoil, Ralph Elliott was gentle and kind. His accusers were not.

*The "Genesis Controversy"* is more than a narrative or interpretation of the Elliott controversy at Midwestern Seminary. It is that, but it is also a kind of autobiographical account of Elliott's pilgrimage. After his career as professor of Old Testament was terminated, he found a home as pastor of American Baptist churches and, in a climate of acceptance and trust, earned the respect of that body of Christians. He had an outstanding ministry as a pastor, speaker, and writer. His last assignment was as provost and dean of Colgate Rochester Divinity School/Bexley Hall/Crozer Theological Seminary.

In *The "Genesis Controversy"* Professor Elliott has attempted to show that his ordeal during the late 1950s and early 1960s was a preliminary chapter in the recently climaxed drama of the takeover of the Southern Baptist Convention by the fundamentalist group led at first by Paul Pressler and Paige Patterson. Elliott's treatment of this theme is minimal, but it is adequate since the present controversy has been so well documented in the press.

Elliott gives some attention to the fact that critics were "lying in wait" when Midwestern Seminary opened in Kansas City, where

Elliott was elected as the first faculty member. These critics attacked other faculty members also, but eventually Elliott became the primary target. With the publication of Elliott's *The Message of Genesis* in 1961 the critics had a document to dissect, and thereafter it was "the Elliott controversy."

Non-Baptists, or non-Southern Baptists, may find it difficult to understand that church-related people—ministers—would be lying in wait to attack the theology of seminary professors. It is incredible that the Southern Baptist Convention, through its Cooperative Program, continues to invest vast sums of money in theological seminaries and at the same time allows sporadic attacks upon professors in the seminaries, often by people who themselves are unqualified theologically. (President Duke K. McCall of Southern Seminary in Louisville referred to his local committee of pastors as "the Tarbucket Committee.")

The critics of Ralph Elliott were diverse in nature. Some were students whose ultraconservative background prompted questions when Elliott taught them Old Testament study methods which had been almost universally accepted decades before. Others of them were disappointed preachers who had believed that they would be on the faculty or staff of the new Southern Baptist seminary in Kansas City. Some were opportunists. Some were just fundamentalists who are easily threatened.

It should be pointed out that Elliott's critics worked in shifts. One individual or group would chase him for a while and then drop out to be replaced by a fresh group. On many occasions, Professor Elliott and President Berquist were physically as well as emotionally exhausted from trying to meet with new individuals and groups with whom they had to work through the entire controversy again and again.

Until the mid-1950s, Central Baptist Theological Seminary in Kansas City, Kansas, which had always been an American Baptist institution, had served both American Baptists and Southern Baptists in that region. Central Seminary had elected trustees from Southern Baptist churches and had many students who were Southern Baptists. When the Southern Baptist Convention embarked on its imperialistic expansion during the mid-1940s, its course inevitably led to the decision that Southern Baptists would not contribute to institutions that the SBC did not control. In the mid-1950s, it was reported that the chairman of the Theological Committee of the Southern Baptist Convention had offered to buy Central Seminary from American Baptists.

When Southern Baptists pulled out of Central Seminary, some of Central's trustees—who were Southern Baptists—worked toward placing the new Midwestern Seminary in Kansas City and became Midwestern trustees. When I went to Midwestern Seminary in the summer of 1959, I found complete acceptance and friendliness from the professors of Central Seminary and never noted any resentment from them toward Midwestern. When Elliott refers to Central Seminary trustees, he is usually referring to Southern Baptist preachers who were formerly trustees of Central and then related to Midwestern. On occasion their previous relationships and subsequent disappointments with some of Midwestern's administrative decisions complicated their relationships with Midwestern. President Millard Berquist determined from the beginning to avoid ill will resulting from that previous conflict and selected no faculty or staff person who had had a part in that event. In fact, it seemed that President Berquist tried to balance the number of faculty members whose background was Southern Seminary with those from Southwestern Seminary.

Throughout *The "Genesis Controversy"* Elliott continues to reflect a deep affection and respect for President Berquist. President Berquist was a truly saintly man who gave of himself to defend Professor Elliott for more than two years. It was only about three weeks before Elliott's dismissal that Berquist yielded to the pressure and read the recommendation to the trustees that called for Elliott's dismissal. One might expect that Elliott would feel betrayed and be bitter, but that was not and is not the case. Elliott never got as angry with Berquist as some of the rest of us did, and he continues to express his affection for him. In the years following the dismissal, Berquist spoke affectionately about Elliott to the rest of us. It is to the credit of both Elliott and Berquist that this attitude prevailed, and to the credit of Berquist that he never punished any of us who protested his part in the "solution" of the Elliott controversy.

Most readers may find it difficult to believe that things can happen this way in an ecclesiastical setting. The peculiar nature of Southern Baptists and the Southern Baptist Convention, however, not only permits but actually encourages such inconsistencies. On one occasion, President Berquist returned to Midwestern from Nashville. He had been to Nashville to seek seminary funding from the Southern Baptist Convention's executive committee. He reported that Porter Routh, then executive secretary/treasurer of the SBC executive committee and another kind and gentle man, in substance had said to him, "Millard, you have to settle this Elliott thing. It is going to cost us a million dollars in the Lottie Moon missions offering." Porter Routh had one agenda; the current SBC president Herschel Hobbs had another; the critics had others. President Berquist was caught in this unbearable pressure from various sources. The question of justice for a professor of Old Testament was not the agenda of the power people.

Early in the controversy at Midwestern, Ralph Elliott told me that he and President Berquist could handle the controversy better if the rest of us would stay out of it. He particularly urged me to talk to Professor G. Hugh Wamble and ask him to refrain from writing letters and articles on the controversy. Berquist and Elliott wanted to contain the controversy and minimize the damage to the seminary, and Berquist was committed to defending Elliott. For this reason we, some of Elliott's colleagues, appeared to be nonsupportive or playing it safe. Elliott did feel abandoned both then and later. About three weeks before Elliott was dismissed, when we learned that President Berquist was supporting a "deal" that would save Elliott with a kind of compromise, some of us wrote letters to the trustees and otherwise went public in support of Elliott. It was too late to help. It may not have helped even if it had been earlier.

When Elliott was dismissed several colleagues published protests and some were even threatened with dismissal. Those I know who spoke openly on Elliott's behalf and against the trustee action were Professors Heber F. Peacock, Alan Gragg, G. Hugh Wamble, William H. Morton, and myself.

Elliott's narrative will be rewarding to anyone interested in

Southern Baptist history, theological education, or persons who have gone on after a severe unjust experience. Elliott never spoke harshly about those who did him in. His natural reticence even prevented him from giving himself a fair statement on some occasions. For example, months before the dismissal, a trustee committee chaired by L. D. Johnson thoroughly investigated the charges against Elliott and in its published report exonerated him. Elliott could have made much more of this in his book.

In like manner, Elliott found it difficult to write the actual account of the dismissal, including the hostility toward him, trustee betrayal, and President Berquist's role.

When the trustee committee made its report, one would have expected the full board to have voted officially to dismiss all accusations and completely acquit Elliott. But, of course, this never happened. The continuing criticism was allowed to deny Elliott the acquittal he deserved.

The "good old boy" system of controlling SBC affairs went to work. One phase of this was a visit by President Berquist and Elliott to Oklahoma City to "confer" with Herschel Hobbs, pastor of Oklahoma City's First Baptist Church and then president of the Southern Baptist Convention. When Elliott discussed this planned trip with some of us, we advised against it. In our naive way, we still held to the notion that trustees governed theological seminaries and that convention presidents had one vote the same as anyone else. Elliott's response to our case was that he could hardly refuse President Berquist who was risking his own career for Elliott. We reasoned that once a professor appeals to or confers with the power people, the issue is automatically changed and no solutions are considered except compromises. Reports indicated that President Hobbs was also committed to saving Ralph Elliott's teaching position at Midwestern but that Elliott would have to "eat humble pie."

The weakest part of The "Genesis Controversy" is, in my opinion, Elliott's failure to more fully discuss the "ten-point compromise" that was developed by the trustees (and, I presume, partly with Elliott's agreement) and that supposedly would have saved Elliott. In the first nine points the trustees conceded the legitimacy of the historical-critical study of the Old Testament (which was not theirs to concede since it was not up for grabs), but the clincher was point 10. Point 10 stated that Professor Elliott would agree not to seek the republication (or reprinting?) of *The Message of Genesis*. If my memory is correct, all copies had been sold and Broadman Press had decided not to print any more copies.

The trustees kept Elliott waiting for hours alone in a room in the Muehlbach Hotel while they deliberated. During a break for the evening meal, Elliott came home and called several colleagues to confer with him. They were Professors Roy L. Honeycutt, Heber F. Peacock, and myself. When we heard the "ten-point compromise" we affirmed Elliott's interpretation that point 10 would be published as his capitulation. Agreeing not to republish the book would be interpreted as enough of a surrender—"eating humble pie"—to hold off if not please the critics, enough perhaps to have saved Elliott's job. But we agreed that this recantation would have destroyed Elliott from within, even if it did save his job, which it probably would not have done.

Elliott's refusal to agree not to republish the book allegedly was the "insubordination" for which he was dismissed. He refused, it was said, "to come to a mutual working relationship with the administration." This was not only hypocritical, it was also absurd. Elliott was no more capable of insubordination than gentle and kind President Berquist was capable of making that charge.

Elliott's dismissal was probably inevitable months before the actual event. Trustees of Southern Baptist seminaries are diverse. Some are competent in theological studies; many are not. Some were chosen for the right reasons, to promote and govern institutions of theological education; some were chosen for purely political reasons. Few of the trustees had experience in dealing with serious matters such as the unspecified charges against Professor Elliott. New trustees are elected during controversies and then participate in the final voting when they have not heard the previous evidence. Trustees serve as accusers, defenders, and jury. Some are more concerned with their political futures than justice for an accused. Some display complete integrity and pay the price for defending a professor who has been unjustly put in jeopardy—but they are few. Elliott had no protection from an accrediting institution because

Midwestern Seminary was a new school. New schools cannot apply for accreditation until they graduate their first class. Usually it takes five years for a school to become accredited. When Midwestern later became accredited by the Association of Theological Schools, it had a tenure statement which would have called for due process. Due process calls for a specific charge to be stated and proved, counsel for the accused, and a clear statement of the action. Elliott was not specifically charged. The issue was, of course, his theological teachings, but he was dismissed for insubordination. He was not afforded counsel during his hearings. When we his friends sat in the hotel lobby at his request, the chairman and vice chairman demanded that he ask us to leave. We left.

At several points in his book, Professor Elliott expresses disappointment that his major seminary professor in particular and his other professors in general offered him no support or encouragement during his long ordeal. These statements are not the whines of a weak person; rather they are the justified statements of disappointment that the teachers who held similar, if not identical, views of Old Testament studies would not stand up and say so.

The saddest note in the entire book is not Elliott's dismissal, as tragic as that was and is for him, his family, and the rest of us. The saddest note in the book is his occasional reference to the "doublespeaking" of seminary professors from his alma mater. Elliott quotes Glenn Hinson who had studied this tendency and in 1988 reported on it to the Historical Commission of the Baptist World Alliance.

Elliott mentioned this tendency on the part of the seminary professors who tried to please everyone and maintain support from all by using doublespeak. They were critical scholars who spoke clearly within a critical tradition when they were with other scholars, but in church and convention settings they sounded as if they agreed with the least-educated persons present. Elliott refers to a running conversation with one of his professors who said Elliott did not communicate. What he meant was that Elliott would not doublespeak.

When Elliott and I were students and young faculty members at Southern Seminary, few of the older professors remained on the scene. There were many younger professors who would not employ deceptive language, but spoke what they perceived to be the truth in whatever setting they were. There were, however, some professors who did employ the safety of the doublespeak. I recall one senior professor whom we all respected, when we insisted that he publish his teachings, responded, "When you publish it, they will get you." Another highly respected scholar and teacher said one day to a group of us, "If they had understood me, they would have fired me." He had spoken and written in such a way that those who would have opposed him did not understand what he really meant. He retired and died with great respect.

I hope Elliott's book will be read widely throughout the Southern Baptist Convention. Surely he has earned his right to be heard. His reflections are helpful. The "Elliott controversy" was the third or fourth chapter, a short chapter, in a large volume of Southern Baptist confusion and injustice. The last ten or twelve years have been filled with particularly tragic incidents in which innocent people have been hurt for life by the actions of zealots, the politically ambitious, the cruel legalists. We have witnessed public beatings, dismissals, forced retirements, and forced compromises. A few years ago we witnessed the doublespeak of all time in the seminary presidents' so-called "Glorieta Statement." The recent SBC "Peace Committee Report" legalized theological oppression and authorized purges, despite the denials of those who wrote it and passed it.

Elliott's book will not solve these problems. But it may help some to understand how one incident of oppression happened. That is, while The "Genesis Controversy" offers few answers, it may help someone to begin asking the right questions. ⸙

—*Morris Ashcraft*
Wake Forest, North Carolina
February 1992

# Introduction

One purpose of this book is to show the continuity between the so-called "Genesis controversy" of the early 1960s and the continuing chaos within the Southern Baptist Convention. This is important because it demonstrates a simmering evil during a long period of time, and it has implications for *every* denomination. I am obliged to write this particular story because it revolved around me, and because I have data in my files available to no other person.

When I reflect on the 1960s and what came to be known as the "Genesis controversy," it seems so long ago. Yet each time I read of the crisis within the Southern Baptist Convention, yesterday and today touch as if they were part of the same time frame. Indeed they are. It is as if long ago I watched a soap opera but had to abandon it for some years, then upon reentry I discovered that I had not missed much and the story line was fully familiar. There is continuity in the way yesterday and today meet, and the marriage of the two reflects similar events within practically every branch of the Christian family. The "handles" of my own involvement and my own evaluations, however, have a prelude.

I turn to that prelude with a sense of confession. The confession centers on the pain that comes when I realize that such extraneous concerns could have absorbed my attention when—during the 1960s—the world was in such chaos and in desperate need of serious witness rooted in the Kingdom of God. Indeed, that is no less true now.

I refer, of course, to issues such as the civil rights struggle. How could I have been so involved in "religious" matters as to be almost oblivious to the more important human issues of freedom and liberation? At a time when Martin Luther King, Jr. and others were searching for the "beloved community," I was part of a denomination that was isolated in a self-destructive fight. Having so recently witnessed tragic and dehumanizing events in Central America, I am embarrassed again that my own and other Baptist energies are being misspent on secondary things.

## Prelude. A Denomination's Child

To understand the story, you must understand something of who I was, who I became, and who I am.

The day in 1949 when I walked onto the campus of the Southern Baptist Theological Seminary in Louisville, Kentucky, was one of the greatest days of my life. That event was the culmination of a dream. It was like stepping on holy ground. A few days after orientation, I was in the seminary library, crouched on one knee looking for a book on a bottom shelf, when someone touched me on the head, and a voice asked, "Are you finding what you need?" I looked up and it was Dr. Ellis Fuller, seminary president. It was as if God himself had spoken to me.

Little did I realize that this time of awe and fantasy would be the portal that ultimately revealed that seminary players are not always angels, that denominational officials are not necessarily as holy and naive as innocence assumes, and that there was a rich ecumenical world out there from which my narrow heritage had shielded me and towards which my early experience had prejudiced me.

## Appreciation

Perhaps those lines suggest something of my roots and project something of my journey. To guess that they refer to something I have thrown away, however, is to make a false assumption.

My seminary days were wonderful days of reading books and memorizing outlines and preaching in student pastorates. Those days, however, only confirmed what I already believed, namely, that Southern Baptists had the last word of truth, and that I was part of an enterprise that was almost God's total answer to the needs of the world.

New perspectives did not begin to develop until I began a graduate program upon completing the basic seminary degree. During those graduate-study days, I began to think for myself, but still within the framework of the wonderful Baptist family of which I was a part.

That religious systems may be politically oriented and subject to power-grabbing use had not yet occurred to me. Occasionally I ran across the names of Crawford H. Toy and his struggles in Old Testament studies, and William H. Whitsitt and the controversies surrounding his name. Crawford Toy, professor of Old Testament at Southern Seminary, was forced to resign in 1879, and later rendered outstanding service as a professor at Harvard University. William Whitsitt, professor of Church History and president, was forced out by those whose beliefs were strongly Landmarkist. That both were forced to resign from the faculty of the seminary only served to confirm my thoughts that there must have been something wrong with their views.

Rooted in such unexamined orthodoxy, I was a grading assistant and then an instructor in Old Testament while completing my graduate work. My driving motivation was to complete my work and become a pastor. I was greatly surprised when Dr. Clyde T. Francisco of the Old Testament department recommended me to President Duke K. McCall and ultimately to the seminary faculty for subsequent election to the faculty by the board of trustees.

## Reality Dawns

It was during my faculty days at Southern Seminary that the reality of politics and struggles within the organization of the faith community began to come into focus. The catalyst was a call from the seminary president to join a small group of faculty members to assist him by providing some "thought-starter" material to trigger his thoughts as he prepared to write the Sunday School lessons for *Broadman Comments,* a commentary on the International Sunday School lessons published by Broadman Press. Before the volume was published, the group was asked to do the same thing for the following year.

Shortly after an agreement had been made to provide such material for the second volume, the first volume came off the press. There was immediate turmoil because the published material was so similar to what faculty members had submitted. Conflict over this issue precipitated a tremendous power struggle within the faculty and with the president. A similar conflict was in the air with reference to a history of the seminary that had been written by Dr. William Mueller, professor of Church History. As a young, new faculty member with absolutely no experience, I had felt honored to be included in the list of those asked to assist the president. But I was appalled to discover what appeared to be unauthorized and unacknowledged use of materials, and even more shocked by the ugly conflict that developed.

I do not know what the outcome for me might have been in connection with these events. Upon reflection, I now suspect my reaction was one of disappointment, pain, and hurt, rather than of reality and determined action. It was as if the Kingdom had fallen, that holy ground had been desecrated. My false and simple view of the nature of Christian community had been wounded, though not destroyed. I fear I was looking for escape rather than either justice or solution. Battle in the religious context was not my "cup of tea." Beyond that, nice Christian people do not fight—or so I thought.

In that context I was a vulnerable candidate, when in the the heat of the battle, Dr. Millard J. Berquist, newly elected president of the recently founded Midwestern Baptist Theological Seminary in Kansas City, contacted me. President Berquist asked whether I was willing to meet him for a conference at the Louisville airport, Standiford Field. I knew he was in the process of gathering a faculty and assumed he wished to speak with me in order to receive both a student's, and now a colleague's, evaluation of Dr. Clyde T. Francisco as a possible faculty member for Midwestern. This was a natural assumption because Dr. Francisco had made it quite clear to me that he was unhappy about many matters at Southern at that time. As his colleague, he had led me to believe he might go to Southwestern Seminary, but of late had spoken to me on numerous occasions of going to Midwestern.

I was completely unprepared when Dr. Berquist invited me to

become the first faculty member of Midwestern. My initial response to Dr. Berquist was that I felt most uncomfortable to be involved in the conversation and indicated that I could not consider the matter unless I was free to discuss it with Dr. Francisco. (This has a bearing on the subsequent "Genesis controversy.")

With Dr. Berquist's permission, my next step was to get in touch with Clyde Francisco and to share with him my conversation with Dr. Berquist. Dr. Francisco indicated he was terribly disappointed, and found it difficult to understand how one who was so recently his own student could be chosen ahead of him. Later, when we both were visiting our relatives in Virginia (we were both natives of Danville), he reiterated to me, with much emotion, the same viewpoint. At the time, the matter was as much an enigma to me as it was to him. As already mentioned, this matter is noteworthy because it becomes relevant in understanding some of the later conflicts regarding my book *The Message of Genesis* and the storm that followed.

# Chapter 1

# Adventure and Publication

A short time before I was elected to the faculty of Midwestern Baptist Theological Seminary, Dr. William J. Fallis, editor for Broadman Press, the book-publishing arm of the Southern Baptist Convention, visited with the faculty of Southern Seminary in Louisville. He indicated that after due consideration, the editors had decided it was time for Broadman to publish something that took into account the use of the critical tools in biblical study. Fallis said that they were looking for authors and manuscripts. Dr. Francisco, chair of Southern's Old Testament department, suggested to me that the two of us collaborate on such a project. He did so because of a serious interest which both of us had in the book of Genesis. I had done some serious study in that area as a result of both class and seminary work with Dr. Francisco.

Time passed, and Dr. Francisco's heavy extracurricular schedule of preaching and teaching in local churches made it difficult for our work to begin. Therefore, when I went to my hometown for a month's vacation, I took some notes with me to see whether I might get the project underway. I borrowed a typewriter in my father-in-law's business office, and within a month's time I had typed the manuscript that became *The Message of Genesis*. With all candor, it was a popularizing of some of my lecture notes. The basic direction of the material had been shaped under Dr. Francisco, who was the primary advisor of my graduate program.

When I returned to Louisville, I showed my manuscript to Dr. Francisco. He kept it for a few days, and upon returning it, suggested that I submit it to Broadman Press. I did so, and the manuscript was accepted. Before the project was completed, however, I moved to Kansas City and began my work with Midwestern Baptist Theological Seminary. The book was published on July 1, 1961.

There was one further preliminary event that was to affect the climate in which the struggle surrounding *The Message of Genesis* took place. As the president of Midwestern sought additional faculty members for the new institution, I reminded him that there were some excellent people who had been released from Southern's faculty because of the feud with their president. These people were capable and experienced, and we had been associated in the *Broadman Comments* project. Four of these men were added to Midwestern's faculty: Morris Ashcraft, theology; William Morton, archaeology; Hugh Wamble, church history; Heber Peacock, New Testament. This certainly did not help relations with Southern Seminary and, as we discovered later, it did not please my Old Testament mentor who appears to have considered these men antagonists.

My recommendation of these people and their subsequent election appears to have been an additional reason for some persons at the older seminary to cast Midwestern in a bad light. In an August 15, 1960 letter, Francisco accused the departed brethren (the twelve who had been dismissed from Louisville) of using the "shock method" technique in teaching and wondered whether I had not been caught up in the infectious nature of the "cause." He also apologized and wrote, "Pray for me that I will not be so sensitive to the old scars of the controversy. It is hard to refrain from being oversensitive when you have once been burned." I do not know exactly what the "old controversy" was, nor do I understand his relationship with the twelve, but these foundational events later entered into attitudes relating to Midwestern's plight and the "Genesis controversy."

Other more immediate events provided fertile opportunity for the weaving of threads from the past into complicating patterns. Some of those threads came from the Kansas City environment.

## A Negative Environment

For many years, the Central Baptist Theological Seminary, an American Baptist institution in Kansas City, Kansas, had been educating students from Southern Baptist churches and for Southern Baptist pastorates. Some Southern Baptists served on Central's board of trustees. There was a certain sense in which the school was jointly sponsored. Because of its role in educating Southern Baptist students, some of Central's trustees sought financial help from Southern Baptists. The official response amounted to, "We do not support what we do not control." This response stimulated a rift. Southern Baptists lost their places on the board of trustees, and since 1956, Central has been singularly related to American Baptists. It was more than coincidence that led to the establishment in 1957 of Midwestern Baptist Theological Seminary in the sister city of Kansas City, Missouri.

## Naive Innocence

I did not know that bit of history at the time I went to Midwestern. I wish I could say that had I known it, I would not have gone to the new school. However, I am not sure that such knowledge would have altered my decision. I have used the phrase "naive innocence," perhaps as a way of trying to salve my own conscience. The truth may be that I had been so brainwashed by the Southern Baptist system that at the time I probably would have concluded that Midwestern was justified because other groups were not rightly preserving the faith and certainly were not bearing enthusiastic witness for the Gospel.

## Early Struggles

Struggles connected with the founding of the new institution also affected its history. Some people formerly associated with Central Seminary indicated they would be willing to serve the new seminary in any capacity, "from janitor to president." It is unlikely anyone really wanted the janitor's job. But the strange thing is that *none* of these people were elected or appointed to *any* position in the new institution, although several were elected to the board of trustees. I soon realized that ecclesiastical struggles leave bitter residues of mistrust. That applications from former Central Seminary personnel were ignored may well have been deliberate. The resentment of former Central people over not being included was immediately focused on the newly elected president of Midwestern Seminary, Dr. Millard J. Berquist, a warm, patient, and compassionate man who was called from the pastorate of the First Baptist Church of Tampa, Florida.

For the most part, the Midwestern trustees who were former Central people, were even more conservative in outlook and far more parochial. Although they may not have been "fundamentalists," they were influenced by the literalist approach to the Scriptures and had serious reservations about the importing of a faculty nucleus from Southern Seminary. It may sound strange today when it appears Southern Seminary is walking a double line so as to stand in good favor with whoever finally wins the struggle for control of the Southern Baptist Convention, but in those days theological education at Southern Seminary was far more liberal and open than it was at Central.

## The Publication

It was in such an atmosphere that a very *moderate* volume, *The Message of Genesis*, was published. As I noted above, the project was begun in Louisville at the request of Broadman Press. Had I been in Louisville when the volume was published, the fallout probably would have been minimal. However, a competitive atmosphere in Kansas City made for a totally different situation. By competitive atmosphere I refer to an emerging struggle as to who was going to control the new seminary and to the "threat" the new institution seemed to be for some in the midwestern section of the country. Many of the pastors there had gotten by without seminary training. A ready supply of seminary graduates could create competition for positions and afford certain threats to security as nonseminary graduates became more conscious of their own inadequate preparation.

## The Thrust

I used only moderate Old Testament critical methods in *The Message of Genesis*. The effort in the book was directed towards an appreciation of the *message* of this and other Old Testament writings. For much too long this portion of the biblical message had been ignored. I was concerned that it become once more a regular portion of our preaching diet.

Like the Old Testament teachers in all Southern Baptist seminaries at the time, I recognized a difference of literary style between chapters 1-11 and 12-50, even as the parables of Jesus and the historical narration in the New Testament are of different literary character, yet devoted to the same inspired purpose of presenting God's revelation. The basic question was not whether the Hebrews did or did not use raw materials borrowed from elsewhere. The emphasis was that whatever materials might have been used, the Hebrew writers wrote with a theological and religious purpose--that of magnifying the sole God as Creator, Lord, and Sustainer of nature and humankind. The ancient world had not known such a witness before. It was the pointing of creation materials toward a new and different understanding and purpose in order to stress that creation is God-breathed and God-driven.

The book was a rather conservative effort. A considerable amount of digression was spent in upholding the historicity of the patriarchs. This was a deliberate disassociation from much of the scholarly position at the time. It was further suggested that the later task of the prophets was to call the people back to a religion that was historical and real. Quite in contrast to Julius Wellhausen, with whose brush I was often painted, I made it clear that the Hebrew heritage was *not* something initiated and concocted to fit a late priestly scheme, but was wrought by God in the history of a people, including and prior to the time of Moses. The historical patriarchs were the spiritual ancestors of the prophetic Moses. The "theological interpretation" of Scripture which I was advocating was a far cry from earlier efforts of mere literary criticism. Although the interpretation of single points in the book was important to me, I was primarily interested in conveying a perspective of interpretation which might help us to more easily reclaim the message of all the Old Testament. The book was very conservative by yesterday's terms. Today, some thirty years later, it looks absolutely anemic in an age that talks about biblical interpretation in terms of the "hermeneutics of suspicion."

## Chapter 2

# The Turmoil

As suggested before, the book *The Message of Genesis* was not introduced into a neutral setting. There were at least four negative factors involved in its reception:

1. seminary rivalry and disappointed faculty personnel;
2. local political rivalry in the old Central Seminary mileau;
3. power grabbing fostered by the Southern Baptist system; and
4. theological differences which may have represented a "mix" in the system from as far back as the General and Particular Baptist heritage.

Only the latter has not been alluded to, but it will receive attention along the way.

### Continuity with the Present Struggle

These four factors suggest an absolute connection between elements of the past and the most recent efforts at Southern Baptist takeover. There is a real continuity between the 1960s "Genesis controversy" era and the present literalisms, power struggles, and theological debates. Tasks were left unfinished, festering, and lingering. Along the way there have been those who—all the while trying to fan the elements into flame—waited patiently, planning towards the *kairos* moment.

### Rumblings

The initial rumblings were there prior to the publication of *The Message of Genesis*. A handful of people from Missouri and Kansas were not willing for Midwestern's President Berquist to have a free hand in the institution. As early as January 25, 1960, Mack Douglas, then pastor of the Tower Grove Baptist Church in St. Louis, wrote to remind President Berquist that "as pastor of a church with the largest Sunday School and Training Union in Missouri, a church that is either in first or second place in cooperative program gifts for many years, and also as chairman of the budget committee of the state," he (Douglas) needed to have a hearing. He went on to indicate that "the rank and file of Southern Baptists, including the present president of our convention, former presidents, and the vast majority of our people, will not tolerate liberalism in our seminaries." This was what we faced almost from the beginning at Midwestern Seminary.

There was then, even before *The Message of Genesis*, a definite thrust to take over the convention and a plan developing to do so by "clearing house" in the seminaries. In that same January 15, 1960 letter, Mr. Douglas wrote:

> I am sure you will agree with me that if Missouri Baptists and others in the Midwestern part of the nation bring strong statements concerning the orthodoxy of certain professors to a convention, say meeting in St. Louis in 1961, that the rank and file of Southern Baptists will vote to clear our ranks of those who are not true to the word of God, and the convention might even go so far as to state that conservatives only should teach in our seminaries.[1]

With that implied threat, Douglas demanded that certain faculty members be made to answer directly before the executive committee and board of trustees of the seminary. It sounds so very much like the jargon used during the last decade and a half within the Southern Baptist Convention. Incidentally, the sharing of such letters with me indicates something of President Berquist's personal commitments and the very close working relationship in those early days.

The tactics used from the beginning were those of the "dirty tricks" variety. They might have been studied by those who were going to perform in the Watergate scandal in our nation's capital.

---

[1]Mack Douglas, letter to President Berquist, 25 January 1960.

When there is a messianic complex and only *you* feel that you can protect God (as though God needs protection), then any method appears legitimate as a means to an end. As early as 1959, two or three students had surrendered excerpts from classroom notes to Mr. Douglas as requested. The criticism, although centered upon Professor William Morton and me, was designed to indicate that Dr. Berquist was not an adequate administrator and was allowing a "liberal" seminary to develop.

It soon became necessary for Berquist, Morton, and me to meet with six of the seminary trustees in an all-day session, in February 1960. Our president recognized that the attack was upon him as much or more than it was upon us, and he took the lead in the meeting. He had already told Morton and me the night before that "if anyone had to leave, he would leave with us," for he felt that our perspective was his, or at least he had confidence in our perspective, and that to dismiss us was to question his leadership.

## Standing Alone

During those early troublesome days, it had been hoped that some official encouragement might come from the other seminaries. From several individual faculty members here and there, there were gracious letters of support and encouragement. However, disappointment and jealousy began to raise their ugly heads.

For instance, I had failed to include any use of a certain professor's book in the Old Testament syllabus at Midwestern. He suggested at that point that it would be better to delay the publication of my book until he could get out a revised edition of his book "to clear the way for mine." This was the same professor who had urged me to submit the manuscript in the first place.

Expediency began to loom large in our basic principles of operation. With the challenge brought by the "power" forces in the St. Louis and Kansas City areas and the innuendos which were coming from past relationships at Southern Seminary, Broadman Press—having initially requested the book—began to encounter some reluctance in the higher echelon in Nashville. The reluctance was born from a fear that the book might get somebody in trouble.

One of the editors shared these fears with another denominational press which had expressed some interest in taking over the publication of the book. Both Broadman and I decided, however, that the primary purpose would be missed if the book were not done by Broadman, because it was written with Southern Baptists in mind. In spite of the political and the theological tensions that were in evidence, both William Fallis and Joseph Green of Broadman Press recommended that the book be published with an early 1961 deadline.

## The Escalation

After the book was published in July 1961, things escalated rapidly. A summary of the scenario will be better served at a later point. What is important here is the beginning of the use of tactics that have continued until the present time.

Some were aware even in those early days that the committee on committees of the Southern Baptist Convention could be subjected to the kind of pressure that might result in getting their own people elected to the board of trustees of Midwestern Seminary. So an "informal" group of some fifty people met at the Capitol Hill Baptist Church in Oklahoma City to plot strategy. The group was composed of people who had already been involved in caucus initiatives in their own states. A primary leader in the group was W. Ross Edwards of Kansas City, secretary of the board of trustees at Midwestern and formerly on the Central Seminary board of trustees. He was one of those who had offered to serve "in any capacity" in the new seminary and appears to have been greatly disappointed in his failure to achieve a more significant post. The purpose of the meeting, as reported by a March 16, 1962 Baptist Press release was "to secure the election of what the group considers theologically conservative men to the trustees of the Kansas City Seminary."

W. Ross Edwards served as convener of the group and released a statement saying that "the meeting was bathed with a spirit of humility and concern over resolving the difficulties within the denomination's organizational framework. It closed with these men on their knees in prayers of dedication." This was not the last time that piety and politics have been joined as allies. The report sounds so very similar to caucuses in more recent years when right-wing Southern Baptist pastors have "been on their knees in prayer" and have come to the conclusion that God has designated a certain one of their number to run for the presidency of the Southern Baptist Convention. It cannot be missed that it was the Edwards caucus of 1962 that authorized the political tactics and the grasping of the committee on committees as an effective takeover action. Paul Pressler, who is credited with the discovery of such a possibility at a later time, simply perfected a strategy he had borrowed from an earlier group. He is often incorrectly named as the "discoverer" of the possibility.

## The Disease Spreads

It is notable that Mack R. Douglas from St. Louis was also at the meeting. Mr. Douglas was at the time a member of the Southern Baptist Sunday School Board, the parent body of Broadman Press, the book's publisher. In January the same year (1962), the Sunday School Board, at its semiannual meeting in Nashville, defended its publication of the book and furthermore "encourages Broadman Press to continue to publish books which present more than one point of view." What is obvious is that the infighting, to take over various organizations from within, had already begun. It was no longer possible to take things at face value. Membership on a board no longer meant advocacy of its mission, but increasingly, it meant political opportunity. Those many years ago, the stage was being set for the present chaos.

It is also of interest that in this same general time frame a name surfaced that has had continuing prominence in Baptist disputes across the years and is of utmost importance in the formation of more recent strategy. On February 13, 1962, Paul Pressler—in more recent years a Texas judge who is generally believed to be the architect of the present political quest for orthodoxy within the Southern Baptist Convention—wrote to Midwestern Seminary's President Berquist, with copies to the chairman of the board of trustees, to Dr. K. Owen White, and to Dr. James Riley of Houston.

In his letter, Pressler referred to the 1925 "Declaration of Faith" of the Southern Baptist Convention and its reference to the Bible as "truth, without any mixture of error." As Nancy Ammerman pointed out in *Baptist Battles*,[2] that phrase is open to various interpretations, but it is obvious Pressler was using the phrase as a strict literalist with a dictation understanding of the inspiration of the Scriptures. Pressler accused me of violating what he called "this basic Baptist tenet," and placed me in the category of "modernists who, while claiming to be friends of the Gospel, undermined it." Since Midwestern received support through the Cooperative Program, he indicated that "as long as Dr. Elliott, or one holding a position such as his, teaches at an institution supported by the Cooperative Program, I shall have an entirely different attitude about my giving to Southern Baptist causes." The letter closed with the following sentence.

> I pray that Dr. Elliott will be quickly dismissed for his denial of the inerrancy of the Scripture.[3]

The reference to the Cooperative Program, often given attention in Southern Baptist life prior to every consideration (or seemingly so to me), was another prelude to more recent tactics. Both the conservatives and the moderates have used the Cooperative Program as a hammer and threat—giving through and withholding from—as the expedient moment and cause conveniently dictate. The elements of that campaign, which began many years ago, have been nurtured across the years with the same organizational threats and the same litmus paper test of the inerrancy of Scripture. When coupled with the Oklahoma group's effort to impose its own slate of trustees, it all sounds very familiar and contemporary.

---

[2]Nancy Ammerman, *Baptist Battles* (New Brunswick NJ: Rutgers University Press, 1990) 65.

[3]Paul Pressler, letter to President Berquist, 13 February 1962.

## A Call to Other Seminaries

During those early days, efforts were made to energize the collective resources of all the seminaries in response. Each of the Southern Baptist seminaries used the same basic approach to Old Testament studies. The same bibliographic resources were available in each of the institutions, and some attention had been given towards developing some uniform placement testing and basic expectations in the various seminary settings. President Berquist attended a meeting of the seminary presidents in early March 1962. He had hoped to find there some strength in solidarity, but returned to report to us that the attitude was, "You must go it alone." The interrivalry was stronger than the common goal.

The situation was also made more difficult because of some of the tensions still remaining over Midwestern's use of faculty who were personae non grata at one of the other seminaries. That state of affairs seems doubly tragic by hindsight. In those days, the seminaries had sufficient standing in the Convention to have honestly indicated that they did not foster an inerrantist philosophy (with exceptions) and to have outlined forthrightly their understanding of the Scripture. Such respected writings as those of W. T. Connor from Southwestern Seminary in Fort Worth and E. Y. Mullins from Southern in Louisville could have been used to buttress the position. Connor's and Mullins's positions were still appreciated and respected traditions at that time. Had the seminaries joined together in candid and honest statement as allies, I very much believe it would have laid the matter to rest. Unfortunately, there seemed to be some feeling that one institution's being "picked off" enhanced another's position.

## Politics over Theology

Issues ultimately were so confused that power politics preceded theology. One detects that this hybrid mixture of power politics and theology continues in the more recent struggles. Personalities and positions engage in combat, and theological theses are called into prominence in order to justify, and at times hide, the basic issues involved. Even a casual reading of the Baptist story from the earliest days will verify that this has always been too prevalent in our history. (Unfortunately, a reading of the history of ecumenical church councils reveals a similar picture.) The matters were far more than those related to a particular person. I shared with many at the time what I wrote in a September 14, 1962 letter to missionary Archie L. Nations in Japan, namely, that it was "the beginning of the destruction of all of our institutions" as we know them. Unfortunately also, that statement has proved to have been prophetic.

A number of people properly analyzed the deeper issues at the time. Paul O. Ebhomielen, a product of Southern Baptist mission work in Nigeria and a student at Midwestern in 1961, wrote a very detailed letter to the members of the board of trustees in which he accurately grasped the larger issues that would plague Southern Baptists in the future. He had been at the seminary only three months when he wrote his letter. His comments are in the context of his surprise that the position of critics "has made it necessary for the board of trustees to meet to decide whether the author of the book has been guilty of heresy." Among his insightful comments are the following.

> Freedom of speech and religion is the right of every citizen of the United States of America. It is enshrined in her Constitution. And even before this constitution was born, Baptists have been known to champion and uphold the principles of religious liberty and freedom of belief. The Baptists in the Foreign Mission fields cherish these beliefs. It is now to be doubted that these attitudes of these critics make room for these beliefs any more.
>
> For instance, there is no Baptist who does not believe that the Bible contains the *inspired* word of God. But opinions differ within this denomination as to the method of inspiration—whether it be mechanical (dictation method), dynamic, or plenary. Yet it will hardly be justifiable for the believers in the mechanical method to make a move to eject the dynamist from the Baptist group simply because the dynamist does not believe just as he believes.
>
> Furthermore, we will be deceiving ourselves to think that problems about the Mosaic authorship of the first five books of the Bible do not exist, or even to disregard the questions arising from the first eleven

chapters of Genesis. One thing is clear, no question or problem about the eternal *message* is conveyed in these books, especially in *Genesis*.

It is therefore my view that any precedent set down now in cracking down on a professor for his views must have a calculated effect on the climate of opinion, not only in Baptist theological seminaries, but also in the Southern Baptist denomination as a whole. Such a precedent can only have the ill effect of stifling the intelligence of the scholars, creating fear of expression, and resulting in denominational retardation. Very soon, the critics will get together a cast or mold of thought for all Baptists. They necessarily would have to tell us what to think and believe and also *how* to think and believe them. This will not be the freedom we have known and loved.[4]

In grasping so perceptively this precedent for current retardation, Mr. Ebhomielen was unfortunately a most accurate prophet. There is another aspect he could not have grasped at that time but which has come to pass nevertheless. This tendency to curtail freedom through one dogmatism or another has caused fallout in the mission program of Southern Baptists. In a recent trip to Central America, I encountered churches in Cuba, for instance, which have withdrawn from the Western Baptist Convention, traditionally related to Southern Baptists. A Cuban professor was dismissed from his seminary post. The non-Baptist denial of freedom is not acceptable to indigenous people. What began within the domestic part of the family in the United States is now affecting international missionary relationships.

## The Matter of Heresy

As related to this matter of power struggle and control, it is interesting that I was not ultimately dismissed from the faculty of Midwestern Seminary because of heresy, but for "insubordination." The matter of insubordination will be explored presently. This discussion of political tensions and the language used in the dismissal action should not hide the fact that there were serious

---

[4]Paul Ebhomielen, letter to Midwestern Seminary board of trustees, copy to the author, 27 November 1961.

theological issues involved. Mr. Ebhomielen, in his letter, rightly perceived that power and theological issues were often intertwined. In a later discussion of the chronology of the Genesis incident, one will even discover that serious theological discussion about the nature of the Scriptures and the nature of theological education led to certain actions and conclusions prior to the dismissal action. Furthermore, none of the comments I make should be taken to imply that many of the people involved were other than sincere in their efforts to rid the convention of what they perceived to be heresy, and, in their sometimes messianic action, "to get the heretic."

During the heat of the struggle, much correspondence came to me from both ordained and unordained people. In studying that correspondence, I find that nearly all of the writers were concerned about the nature of the biblical revelation and the integrity of the Scriptures. The great surprise is that more than ninety percent of the letters from so-called "lay" people in the churches is supportive and appreciative. The disconcerting factor, on the other hand, is that approximately the same percentage of letters from clergy was extremely critical. An attempt to "defend the Bible" appears to have brought out the worst in clergy-types. Often their letters were vitriolic, caustic, and at times even sexually suggestive. (My impression was, and is, that there are a lot of sick people in the "professional" ministry.) The point is, however, that the issue of "heresy" and concern for biblical integrity was at the center of the struggle. Even those whose roots were in the earlier political situation that helped in part to give birth to Midwestern, regardless of their motivation, centered their campaign around the biblical issue.

## Our Heritage

This is certainly in keeping with our heritage as a Baptist people. In more recent times, I have served as chairperson of the Commission on Denominational Identity for American Baptists. In this particular project, I have analyzed responses from the right, the left, and the in-between. There is still consistency in the clamor of Baptist people that the Bible be recognized as the cradle of our existence. The Bible has always been at the center of Baptist life. Our greatest controversies have taken place here at all points in our history. Unfortunately, strife over the Bible and its corresponding divisiveness has often presented a sordid picture for both the Christian and the non-Christian world. Nonetheless, even in fragmentation, even at times superstitiously so, the Bible has been at the center. This allegiance to the Bible, and this debate, has been in every part of our existence from John Smyth to the present. Even the so-called Baptist liberals like John Clifford and Harry Emerson Fosdick have built their cases upon a particular view of the Bible. But in such struggles it was the Bible that was important, as is evident in the seriousness of attention given in, for example, Fosdick's two books, *The Modern Use of the Bible* and *Guide to Understanding the Bible.*[5]

## The Genesis Focus

On all sides, the major question in the "Genesis controversy" was how best to keep the spotlight on the Bible and allow it to be a central authority in our life and mission. Is the Bible *a* central authority or *the* central authority? In the center of the storm, those of us who were actors in the storm, from whatever vantage point, had at least one thing in common: a concern for the integrity of the Scriptures. Some antagonists were, of course, not willing to acknowledge this. Because biblical criticism was involved in my Genesis studies, especially Pentateuchal criticism, critics always seemed spontaneously to bring to mind Julius Wellhausen with whom they associated a destruction of Scripture and a minimization of inspiration. Perhaps it was this earnest concern for Scripture that so deafened their ears and clouded their vision that they refused to give any attention to my academic address at Midwestern (the first in a series, required of every elected faculty member), which had as its central thrust "Beyond Biblical Criticism." They would have

---

[5]For amplification, see "American Baptists: A Unifying Vision, a Background Resource Document," produced by the American Baptist Commission on Denominational Identity, *American Baptist Quarterly* 6/2 (June 1987).

found in that address many things that agreed with their own criticisms and might have discovered many commonalities. The center of the concern was the Bible.

As a matter of fact, it has been personally comforting to discover that in more recent years, directions set in my concern to go "beyond biblical criticism" have been developed by numerous scholars in an attempt to correct the deficit.

But as always, the concern was shredded into what was considered by the orthodox as truth or heresy. Part of this had to do with Christology and how the Bible relates to the centrality of Christ. That is still a major part of the ongoing issue, as Morris Ashcraft, a faculty member at Midwestern in the 1960s, and later dean at Southeastern Baptist Theological Seminary, outlined so well in an excellent article written in the midst of the latest Southern Baptist struggle. Prior to resigning from the deanship at Southeastern because of the right-wing takeover there, he wrote an article entitled "Revelation and Biblical Authority in Eclipse." Ashcraft makes a distinction between the ultimate authority, God, as made known through Jesus Christ, and the immediate authorities—"the church, which embodied and preserved the tradition of the revelation, and the Scriptures, which preserve and communicate the mighty acts of God." He decries what he calls the "reversal of the ground of authority."[6]

This "reversal of authority" was inherent in the 1960s' debate. When there is a reversal of the ultimate authority and the intermediate authority, then it is necessary to build all kinds of defenses for the Bible as the ultimate authority, on the subterranean suspicion that if any iota of the Bible falls, its entire message loses credibility. The inevitable result is the building of propositions about the Bible that serve as a Maginot line to protect the Bible. It was so then; it is so now.

---

[6]Cf. Morris Ashcraft, "Revelation and Biblical Authority in Eclipse," *Faith and Mission* 4/2 (Spring 1987) 9.

## The Inerrancy Issue

The inerrancy issue is, of course, not new in Baptist life. Southern Baptists in particular fought a hard battle that led to the adoption of "The Baptist Faith and Message" statement in 1925. What was new in the beginning of the 1960s was that nobody, other than those involved with Midwestern Seminary, made any serious effort to deal with the matter. The issue therefore gained momentum, and its supporters gained the kind of encouragement to contribute to a continuing effort. As C. R. Daley expressed it in a *Western Recorder* editorial, "Elliott Goes, Problem Remains."[7]

Not only did the problem remain, it gained such sufficient strength as to divide the family into the "orthodox" and the "heretics," with the Bible as the battleground. This was the theme that ran throughout the period of the "Genesis controversy" and continues until now. The book was published in July 1961 and the orthodoxy-heresy issue became so intense that by the end of 1961, one editor wrote:

> It's strange how those who sometimes have the most to say about Baptist freedom use the privilege carelessly themselves. Frankly, we're growing a bit weary of those who are endeavoring to pour all of us into their own little theological mold. It is contrary to a Baptist belief that we hold dear—the right to interpret the Scriptures in our own way under the leadership of the Holy Spirit.[8]

Later we will look more closely at the nature of my particular event and the issues involved. At this point, let me say that long years of reflection on the struggle and an analysis of the emphases and styles involved, lead easily to the conclusion that the true heretics—notwithstanding the use of very orthodox terminology—are those who search for nonexistent "original autographs." These are the same people who demand a rational,

---

[7]Cf. C. R. Daley, "Elliott Goes, Problem Remains," *Western Recorder*, 8 November 1962, 8.

[8]Marse Grant, editorial: "Why Seminary Professors Don't Write Many Books," *Biblical Recorder* 127/44 (11 November 1961).

human-centered theology that is based upon *what* you believe concerning theories *of* and *about* the Bible, as opposed to a God-centered, experiential *whom* you know. The inerrantist theology requires one to muster up a power to "protect" the Bible as though its longevity and use depend upon an ability to protect what you have. This approximates hubris, self-centeredness, that worst sin and the greatest heresy. Good intentions bring protective Bible overlays, like goldsmiths overlaying their work with gold and casting for it silver chains. The work remains an idol nonetheless (Isaiah 40:18-20). The same human-centered direction raises the inanimate Bible beyond the animate Christ. Such a displacement of Christ needs to be called by the double words of heresy and sin.

Some people thought at the time that we would recognize the heresy for what it was, and they found "encouragement in the hope it is somewhat of a growing pain we are suffering and that in just a few more years there will be maturity . . . the situation will soon improve or 1962 will go down as the year of tragedy for Southern Baptists."[9] Since we did not handle the issue for what it was, my own judgment at the time was echoed by C. R. Daley, who wrote that "the Year 1962 could well be remembered as the year of major directional changes for Southern Baptists."[10] Furthermore, Daley added, speaking of Midwestern's trustees:

> They must know by now that Elliott is not a glaring example of heresy among a host of safely orthodox teachers in our seminaries. If he is a heretic, then he is one of many and indeed is not at the head of the line. Professors in all our seminaries know Elliott is in the same stream of thinking with most of them, and is more in the center of their stream than most of them.[11]

Unfortunately, some of the worst fears of the time have come true. One wonders whether we may see the twilight of a denomination on the horizon as campaigns develop for searching out the heretics.

---

[9]John J. Hurt, in *The Christian Index,* 27 September 1962.
[10]C. R. Daley, "A Decision of Destiny," *Western Recorder,* 27 September 1962.
[11]Ibid.

But before leaving these early intimations of turmoil and the reflections on continuing struggle, it is in order to suggest that such seed sown in any denomination appears to produce the same disease. I have been speaking primarily about Southern Baptists. But the inerrantist disease built upon politics over theology, sustained by charges of heresy, and culminating in division is not peculiar to Southern Baptists. The same pressures with similar results have been known elsewhere.

When the 1960s' furor over my own critical approach to the Old Testament began, I was in regular conversation with a New Testament scholar who was teaching at a Missouri Synod Lutheran seminary. He initiated the contact, perhaps as a kind of conversational therapy because he himself was under a similar attack for his New Testament work. He actually found it necessary to face synodical reprimand. One day I received a rather strange telephone call from him in which he said, "Ralph, you won't be hearing from me anymore; it isn't safe to be in conversation." He went on to indicate that I should remember that he had appreciation for my views and stood in much the same place, but necessity was leading in another direction. I did not hear from him anymore, but I did watch from afar. His denomination, the Missouri Synod Lutheran Church, engaged in the same kind of destructive campaign over the inerrancy issue. A seminary was basically destroyed and faculty persons went into exile. To help "save the seminary and the denomination," my friend appears to have surrendered what I know were private views, but it did not save the denomination from painful disease and serious division. Wherever and whenever sterile orthodoxy with propositions *about* the Bible is promised over warm relationships created through experiential biblical faith, turmoil inevitably is the result.

Chapter 3

# The Roots of the Struggle and Continuity

Two themes are woven into this brief recital of events. One has to do with the continuity of the struggle up to the present time. The other has to do with the nature of the struggle as focused on a continuing attempt to understand the character of the Bible. Delineation of both these themes is necessary if the development of the struggle between groups whose roots are in another time is to be understood.

## The Theme of Continuity

Paul Pressler, a federal judge in Houston, Texas, is well known as the architect of current strategies to capture the leadership of the Southern Baptist Convention. (Pressler's work and influence were the subject of a public television documentary by Bill Moyers.) Pressler is credited with having discovered the strategy for electing a president of the Convention who could in turn have a significant impact on every appointment within the convention and, in time, completely dominate the direction of Southern Baptist life.

Judge Pressler certainly perfected the political use of the committee on committees in the election of trustees favorable to his cause. He was not the first, however, to discover the possibilities of this tactic. He merely built upon an earlier strategy used by a nucleus of Midwestern trustees to gain trustee replacement favorable to their cause. This was the basis of the 1962 "Oklahoma caucus," mentioned above, where the strategy was developed to use the "Genesis controversy" as a cause celebre for capturing leadership at Midwestern. Although the strategy has been fully operative only since 1977, it is the continuation of a concern and a vision for orthodoxy that Pressler himself had entertained as early as 1962.

The "Genesis controversy" caused Pressler great distress and he expressed his concern before Second Baptist Church in Houston, where he was a member, and in a letter to Midwestern's President Berquist. Pressler's theme in his letter dated February 13, 1962 related to the 1925 "Declaration of Faith" of the Southern Baptist Convention and in particular to the portion that speaks of the Bible as "truth without any mixture of error." In his letter, Pressler refers to his wife's heritage and to his own, in order to establish his Baptist ancestry. He states that

> For five or six generations my family have [sic] been leaders in the work of Texas Baptists. I am devoted to the principles for which they have stood and which the Bible teaches. Because of this, as long as Dr. Elliott or one holding a position such as his, teaches at an institution supported by the Cooperative Program, I shall have an entirely different attitude about my giving to Southern Baptist causes.

Pressler then indicated his prayer that "Dr. Elliott will be quickly dismissed for his denial of the inerrancy of the scripture."[1]

James Riley, who at the time was pastor of Houston's Second Baptist Church, wrote to me about Pressler on August 8, 1962, and described him as "a dedicated and zealous young Christian . . . sincerely interested in the work of the Lord."[2] I had no reason then and have no reason now to question that evaluation, although I have serious questions about some of those with whom Mr. Pressler has associated across the years. The point is there is definite and traceable continuity between the Southern Baptist controversy of 1962 and that raging now. The controversy was not addressed from a standpoint of strength available at that time, and now the tables have been reversed. The climate that has been both fostered and captured by the Reagan and Bush political administrations has affected every aspect of life. It has especially provided an environ-

---

[1]Cf. Paul Pressler, letter to President Berquist, 13 February 1962.
[2]James Riley, letter to the author, 8 August 1962.

ment in which right-wing and extremely orthodox religious views and people have had a field day. This climate has nurtured attacks upon good people and good institutions and has encouraged Mr. Pressler and many others.

Obviously I feel that the combined institutions, primarily seminaries, made a serious mistake in not collectively addressing the issue in 1961-1962. It has taken that long for the present thrust to reach fruition.

Mr. Pressler's efforts, however, serve to indicate that there have been seriously divergent viewpoints within Baptist life from our very earliest beginnings. These conflicting viewpoints were thrown into close proximity of contest and struggle when the Southern Baptist Convention was organized in 1845, and they were particularly at war with each other during the formative days of the Southern Baptist Theological Seminary. No doubt this accounts for Southern Seminary's ambiguous position. The difference today is that the failure to engage in serious confrontational theological debate in the early 1960s so emboldened the fundamentalist camp that it began a campaign to "seek it all," whereas cohabitation had been the pattern in earlier years.

Both the right and the left wings of the controversy today are tempted to call each other "non-Baptists" for championing a position the other does not accept. It would be closer to transmitted Baptist tradition to suggest that the Baptist stream has contained threads of varying roots from European soil. The "non-Baptist" element is that of reading each other out of the family in the insistence upon a strictly monolithic approach to things.

The intimations above suggest not only a continuity of thirty years, but a continuity from the founding days of the Southern Baptist Convention and the founding days of Southern Seminary, the mother seminary of all Southern Baptist seminaries. Almost thirty years removed from the "Genesis controversy," I have come to understand the primary significance of history, both in shaping and in creating additional history and in evaluating that history. Because I believe the history of both of the institutions just mentioned contributed so very much to the situation in 1961-1962 and to the present chaos in the Southern Baptist Convention, I want to

examine that rootage as a matter of perspective. Those roots may
have been a causal factor to the elements that have surfaced from
1962 to the present. This should likewise serve as a reminder to all
denominational groups that division of ecclesiology and polity bear
both negative and positive fruits into the distant future.[3]

Diverse threads were pulled into the weaving of the garment
called Southern Baptists. These threads are European in origin, the
General and the Particular Baptists. They are likewise American in
nature, the Regular and the Separate Baptists. I suspect it is impossible for anyone to distinguish these tangled threads with complete
satisfaction. But that the threads are there, and that they are tangled,
and that they are part of today's picture, few will deny.

General Baptists were more Armenian in tone, stressed a general
atonement for all, and underscored a personal confession of faith
and believer's baptism. Particular Baptists were more strictly
Calvinistic and taught a "particular" atonement, Christ having died
for certain elect ones only. These latter Baptists were much less
insistent on everyone being immersed and were more ecumenical in
their relationships.[4] By the time the Southern Baptist Convention
was organized in 1845, these European streams had so intermingled
that a local group might have incorporated certain elements from
both groups so that there were few pure strains.

One should add to this confusion that division in the colonies
which we know as the Regular and the Separate Baptists. The
Regulars are reputed to be rooted in what has come to be known as
the "Charleston Tradition," which was more orderly in a stated
concern for liturgy, worship, theology, and education. The Separates
are rooted in what has come to be known as the "Sandy Creek

---

[3]Two resources have been helpful to me in this regard. See H. Leon McBeth,
*The Baptist Heritage* (Nashville: Broadman Press, 1987) and William Ellis, "A Man
of Books and a Man of the People." E. Y. Mullins and the Crisis of Moderate Southern
Baptist Leadership (Macon GA: Mercer University Press, 1985). Also see an
unpublished paper by E. Glenn Hinson, "Between Two Worlds—Southern
Seminary, Southern Baptists, and American Theological Education," offered to
the Historical Commission of the Baptist World Alliance, 1988.

[4]Norman H. Maring and Winthrop D. Hudson, *A Baptist Manual of Polity and
Practice* (Valley Forge PA: Judson Press, 1963) 12-13, 38-41.

Tradition," which was more evangelistic, revivalistic, and inerrantist in preference, and less concerned about the niceties of theology except as to defend propositional religion. From this mixture, it is possible to encounter varied claims about the Baptist heritage. Different strands have found their way into local churches and in geographical groupings of churches. Various claims for authenticity have always been heard.[5]

The institutional difficulties in serving a people so varied and so mixed were recognized immediately. William E. Ellis paints a very clear picture of the controversies regarding theological education during the long presidency (1899–1928) of E. Y. Mullins at Southern Seminary.[6] Glenn Hinson traces the perception of James Petigru Boyce, guiding hand in the founding of Southern.[7] In an effort to please all and to maintain the support of all, Hinson suggests, seminary personnel from the very beginning spoke according to the needs and perceptions of a particular group. Professor Hinson reminds us of a certain "doublespeak"[8]—specifically, to speak one way in class and another way elsewhere—which has been part of the approach from the beginning. Dr. Boyce wanted to push academically as far as possible but he leaned towards a strategy that pleased the churches. Perhaps that was initially a good strategy for gaining acceptance for a trained ministry. Unfortunately, the seed sown in that day has grown an evil fruit.

"Doublespeak" has become an insidious disease within Southern Baptist life. Through the years, the program at Southern Seminary has acquainted students with the best in current research in the given fields of study. Often, however, this was done with an eye and ear for the "gallery" and how much the "church trade" would bear. Professors and students learn to couch their beliefs in acceptable terminology and in holy jargon so that although thinking one thing, the speaker calculated so as to cause the hearer to affirm something else. When I taught at Southern Seminary years ago, we

---

[5]McBeth, *The Baptist Heritage,* 216, 227-29, 233-34.
[6]Ellis, *"A Man of Books,"* see e.g. 107-10.
[7]Hinson, "Between Two Worlds."
[8]Ibid., 5.

often said to one professor who was particularly gifted at this "doublespeak" game, that if the Southern Baptist Convention should split, he would be the first speaker at both new conventions.

One of the serious difficulties for me personally during the "Genesis controversy" was a running debate with a particular Southern professor who constantly counselled me to use the doublespeak technique. When the difficulties came, he said he believed the same thing on these issues, but I got into trouble and he did not because I did not know how to communicate. What he meant was that I did not know how to doublespeak. My contention was that I got into trouble because I sought to communicate an unambiguous message, and so we never found agreement.

It is my personal belief that this doublespeak across the years has contributed to a lack of nurture and growth and is a major factor in the present problems. The basic question is one of integrity rather than the gift of communication.

There is likewise something about the political structure of Southern Baptist life—perhaps simply its size—that causes young theologians to become ambitious towards being elected or promoted to one post or another. The power game becomes so intense as to sublimate the servant imperative. During the 1980s and the current right-wing climate in America, the Sandy Creek and Separate Baptist strains have found such popular acceptance that plainspeaking rather than doublespeaking became the tactic of the right wing. The general effort that began in the 1960s has now found it much easier to sprout and grow. The 1960s were the pendulum years that enabled the conflict of the pre-1960s to gain momentum and ascendancy. There is a pre- and a post-1960s continuity.

## The Presence of the Demonic

Power has within it, however, a sense of the demonic. Many of the people who become involved in these theological debates are totally sincere in the beginning and motivated by what they believe to be theological and doctrinal mandates of a sina qua non quality. It is a heady thing to taste some sense of victory in one of these theological struggles. It is then that people, even on the same side, begin to engage in power struggles, against the enemy or even against each other. During the decade of the 1980s a number of the "moderate" candidates for the presidency of the Southern Baptist Convention had the same theological commitments as the "conservative" (fundamentalist) candidates. The allegiances are drawn on the basis of power commitments rather than on the basis of theological commitments. The gamesmanship demands, however, that theological and religious jargon be used to camouflage the power or organizational struggle.

It was no different in the 1960s. As a matter of fact, people changed sides again and again, depending on where they thought the winning hand lay. Some of those who ultimately became the leaders in demanding my ouster were initially the leaders in championing my cause when it appeared that success in the battle lay in a different direction. Knowing firsthand the list of players in the 1960s game, I know that some of those who currently are leaders of the "moderate" side were formerly leaders of the "conservative" (fundamentalist) side. One must conclude that the religious power game is similar to the political power game whether played in the governmental setting of the nation's capital or someplace else.

The bottom line is that the political and theological ingredients have had continuity since the beginning days of Baptist life in America, even as in the days of its European origin. What makes present-day events of special interest is the germination of a struggle—using such ingredients—that was launched during the 1960s. Judge Paul Pressler is a visual symbol of that continuity.

## The Theme of Revelation

If one thesis has to do with continuity, the other has to do with revelation, that is, with the nature of the Bible in contrast to propositional religion. Theoretically, the battle has been and is over the nature of the biblical revelation, the Bible itself, or at least over statements *about* the Bible.

To mention Baptists, no matter where on the historical continuum, is to mention the Bible, for the Bible has been central to Baptist existence. Any statement of Baptist distinctives from whatever age will include some reference to the Bible (often primarily the New Testament) as the supreme authority of faith and practice. The emphasis has often been reactionary, a reaction against, for example, a tradition that champions the primacy of Rome or the statements of the Anglican Church. Nevertheless, the Bible was viewed as central. Baptist theological, ecclesiastical, and ethical statements have nearly always been prooftexted by biblical affirmations. The Bible has been the scale by which every facet of Baptist life has been weighed.

In the earliest days in the 1600s when John Smyth was describing the church's worship in Amsterdam, he made it very clear that the Bible was at the center of worship when he said:

> We begin with a prayer, afterward read some one or two chapters of the Bible, give the sense thereof and confer upon the same; that done, we lay aside our books and after a solemn prayer made by the first speaker, we propoundeth some text out of Scripture and prophesieth out of the same by the space of one hour or three quarters of an hour.[9]

From that day to this, the Bible has been used and misused as the key to Baptist life, mission, and thought.

Unfortunately, although maintaining the centrality of Scripture in their lives, Baptists have never been able to agree on what the Bible is and how it came to be. Baptist Walter Rauschenbusch, father of the Social Gospel movement, affirmed the authority of the Scriptures for himself and other Baptists, but lamented that Scripture was often paralyzed by being turned into a law book and a collection of prooftexts, that Baptists fussed about trifles and missed the greatest things.[10]

These Baptists have not, however, considered their biblical understanding to involve trifles. As mentioned elsewhere, serious stresses and strains about the nature of the Bible forced Professor C. H. Toy from the faculty of Southern Seminary as early as 1879. The question then, during the 1960s, and today, involved a literalistic

---

[9]As reported in H. Wheeler Robinson, *Life and Faith of the Baptists* (London: The Kingsgate Press, 1946) 96.

[10]Walter Rauschenbusch, "Why I Am a Baptist," *The Rochester Baptist Monthly* 20 (1905-1906), available in the Ambrose Swasey Library, Colgate Rochester Divinity School/Bexley Hall/Crozer Theological Seminary.

approach to the Bible and the assumption that somewhere back of it all were "original autographs," which if found would be letter-perfect without any mixture of error or variation on whatever the subject, and that any "seeming" problems or contradictions in our present texts would be clarified by such originals.

I remember an occasion during the early 1960s when I had been given a command appearance to meet with critics and answer a series of questions, much on the order of an inquisition. When I pointed out some problems in the Scriptures, my examiner exploded, red in the face, and asked, "But don't you agree that there would be no problems in the original autographs?" Thinking of the oral transmission of tradition and Scripture material over a long period of time before anything was placed in writing, I replied that I was not sure there were any "original autographs."

By original autographs, defenders usually have in mind something dictated word-for-word and absolutely authoritative. In the last analysis, however, it is not the Scripture that is authoritative, but someone's propositional statement about what they believe the Scriptures to be. Two things occur to me in this connection. The first is that it seems so ridiculous to speculate about nonexistent autographs. It is a debate that cannot be won. Since no autographs are available, why spend so much energy with such fragmenting results? To rely on nonexistent autographs suggests a lack of confidence in the reliability of the Scriptures that are available. What I want to know is whether the copy of the Scriptures available to me is reliable. The testimony from my personal experience is strongly affirmative. The second reflection, as already stated above, is that to rely on a propositional statement *about* the Scriptures is the greatest heresy of all. Rationalistic religion, which requires a mental check mark to propositional statements, is quite foreign to experiential and relational biblical religion.

Previously I referred to my former colleague Morris Ashcraft's suggestion that the question was and is an authority question.[11] I

---

[11]Morris Ashcraft resigned as dean of the faculty at the Southeastern Baptist Theological Seminary in 1988, but kept his professorship. His resignation was a protest to the mandates of the fundamentalist trustees who captured the

agree with Ashcraft that Christ is the ultimate authority, and to place immediate authorities above the ultimate authority is to reverse priorities. This is blatant heresy.

It was my personal contention during those controversial days at Midwestern Seminary that Jesus assumed authority over the Scriptures when he made it clear that he had come to "fulfill" the Scripture in the sense of bringing it to completion (*plēróō*). This incarnational fulfillment of the principles that underlay the legalistic system of the time involved modification and change. Obviously Jesus did not subscribe to a literalistic understanding of the Old Testament. Neither did the writers of the New Testament. A comparison of Matthew 2:15 with Hosea 11:1 indicates there was a very free "association of principle" as redemptive principles are made clear in the life of Jesus. Both Jesus and the New Testament writers reshaped tradition and liberated its meaning. Helmut Thielicke thus called Jesus the compass for understanding, with the suggestion that the compass becomes our authority.[12] Hans Kung likewise speaks of "journeying by compass."[13] This implies that Jesus is the ultimate authority, an authority received through experience as one journeys in understanding. That is, it rightly suggests that Jesus interprets the Bible, rather than the Bible being the ultimate interpreter of Jesus.

Fundamentalists, both of the Roman Catholic and the Protestant variety, and specifically Southern Baptist ones, however, added another tier to the tower of authority. Theirs is an authority that involves a literalistic understanding of the Bible, thus controlling the understanding of Jesus. These three levels—proposition, Bible, and then Jesus—relegate the authority of Jesus to the lowest place: proposition controls the Bible, the Bible controls Jesus. Such was the essence of the debate in the 1960s and that debate has persisted in continuity to the most recent crisis in Southern Baptist life.

---

institution's board. Shortly thereafter he retired.

[12]Thielicke made this suggestion in his lecture "Norms and the Problem of Casuistry in Evangelical Ethics" at the Second International English Theology Seminar, 1970.

[13]Hans Kung, *The Church* (New York: Sheed and Ward, 1967) 333.

In January 1988, I spoke at a convocation at Carson Newman College (my alma mater) in Jefferson City, Tennessee. A critic who was present wrote a critique that was published in the *Baptist and Reflector*, the state newspaper of Tennessee Southern Baptists. In the critique, he traced the continuity of the issue and suggested that the college was misguided, asking in a rhetorical way, "Although Elliott is a CNC grad, if he had scarlet fever, would we expose students to him before a cure had been effected?" It was an affirmation that the problem *then*—the 1960s—is the problem *now*.[14]

The authority question has become so intertwined with ecclesiology and power that it is difficult to know which is the driving issue—the question of authority or the relish of the power struggle. Although initially the defense of a particular understanding of revelation may have initiated a power grab in its defense, one suspects the taste of power was intoxicating. Today the theme of revelation appears to be an excuse and smoke screen for wielding and maintaining power.

There seems to be little question but that the roots and the fruits are of the same tree.

---

[14]*Baptist and Reflector* 154/6 (10 February 1988).

# Chapter 4

# The Genesis Event

It is now time to summarize the catalytic event. This so-called "Genesis event," in and of itself, may be important more for what it symbolized than for what it was. Controversies in religion are nothing new in human history. Battle lines have been drawn too many times over the nature of the biblical revelation. This certainly was not the first time the Book of Genesis had been the focal point of controversy; unfortunately, it also was not the last. Yet there was something about this particular dispute that caused it to attract an unusual amount of public attention and to make waves far beyond the religious group within which it occurred.

Although *The Message of Genesis* was not published until July 1961, it was already listed in December 1961 as one of the top news stories of the year. In a poll conducted by Baptist Press, the Southern Baptist Convention news agency, the "Genesis controversy" was listed barely behind first place as the second most significant story of the year. It was called a "doctrinal" issue, and was the larger umbrella under which professors from two seminaries—Southern Baptist Theological Seminary in Louisville and Midwestern Baptist Theological Seminary in Kansas City—were listed as suspect. Within another year, it was the feature on the religion pages of both *Newsweek* and *Time* magazines. Students and editors immediately sensed an issue larger than the immediate dispute. I pointed out above that Nigerian student Paul O. Ebhomeilen, at that time in this country for only three months, viewed the struggle as a "precedent for retardation."

C. R. Daley, editor of the *Western Recorder*, the news publication of the Kentucky Southern Baptists, wrote about the situation on a number of occasions, calling the issue "A Decision on Destiny" in his September 27, 1962 editorial.[1] Daley built his editorial around a statement that Southern Baptist Convention President Herschel H. Hobbs had made that year at the meeting of the Southern Baptist Convention in San Francisco. In part, Daley said:

> The statement of Southern Baptist Convention President Herschel H. Hobbs that decisions affecting our convention for a generation may well be made the next eleven months is not only true but may come in years ahead to be regarded as an understatement. The year 1962 could well be remembered as the year of major directional changes for Southern Baptists.[2]

As suggested earlier, however, the issue was "larger than itself," and larger than Southern Baptists. It serves as something of a prototype for all individuals and all judicatories and denominations whose energies are consumed by ugly debate. It becomes a mirror in which one may find the loneliness of rejection by friends, the demonic nature of public attention even when it is negative in scope, the tragic pressure of political gamesmanship, and the ambiguity of politics in the community of faith. It is a mirror in which one may find the destruction of both institutions and individuals. What happened to a number of students is in itself a study in pathos. Hopefully, the telling of the evil story in larger detail may serve as a warning lest other individuals and groups find themselves in a quicksand that smothers vitality and fragments life. Telling the story will suggest its message, but an illustrative pause is in order so as to sense institutional, ecumenical, and personal implications.

## Illustrative Implications of the Story

People at times surrender institutions under the assumption that such temporary surrender will ultimately preserve the institution. Such was the understanding of Midwestern Seminary's President Millard Berquist.

---

[1]Daley, "A Decision of Destiny," *Western Recorder*, 27 September 1962.
[2]Ibid.

Midwestern had an extraordinary beginning. Almost immediately upon its establishment, a fine quality of academic work was being done and there was a tremendous air of spiritual depth in the community. Midwestern was becoming an embodiment of William Rainey Harper's ideal of wedding together head and heart in the education and training of ministers.[3] More than one-third of Midwestern's student body was composed of mission volunteers.

Initially, President Berquist fought the invasion of his prerogatives in directing the institution. He took the lead in responding on my behalf to all of the attacks concerning the Genesis material. Day and night he spent himself and his energies in maintaining the direction that had been set. The pressure continued to build, however, and President Berquist was greatly affected by the persuasions of then SBC President Herschel H. Hobbs.

Two meetings were of particular importance. The first was a kind of "setting-the-stage meeting" when Dr. Hobbs invited President Berquist and me to be his dinner guests at a Kansas City steak house. At that meeting Dr. Hobbs made it clear that he was "our friend" and that he had the best interests of the institution at heart.

It was the second meeting that was fateful. Dr. Berquist and I were asked to meet with Dr. Hobbs in his study at the First Baptist Church of Oklahoma City. It proved to be a terrible day. The tone of the argument was that we should capitulate to the critics in order to save the institution. From then on, everything was different. Dr. Berquist and I were traveling by automobile and we talked nonstop on the return journey to Kansas City. Upon arriving in Kansas City, we drove to my home and sat in my living room to continue the conversation. Dr. Berquist reached the conclusion that "saving the institution" was dependent upon our "giving in." I strongly affirmed that to do so was a serious mistake. I suggested that the institution would deteriorate and that Dr. Berquist would, in effect, never be the "real" president again. As we stood together, he put his arm around me, and in tears said, "Ralph, we are going to end

---

[3]William Rainey Harper (1856-1906), a Northern (American) Baptist, was the founder and first president of the University of Chicago and its divinity school.

on different sides of this matter."

The personal separation was very painful, but even more painful was the fate of the institution. The declining nature of the institution is now history. My personal friendship with Dr. Berquist continued. Several years after my dismissal from the faculty, we met for lunch when I made a brief visit to Kansas City. He was tired and worn, and still president in name. His comment was, "Ralph, you were right. I haven't really been president of the seminary since that day, and can hardly wait until my retirement." Unfortunately his was not the only sad destruction resulting from a situation that violated personal integrity.

## The Story

The particular narrative will suggest its own larger implications. If you have read the recent book about power struggles in the nation's capital, *The Power Game* by newsman Hedrick Smith,[4] you will note many similarities.

### 1. Pastor-Student Collusion

Rumblings at Midwestern Seminary began as early as 1960. The first attack, as already indicated, was by Mack Douglas, the politically oriented pastor of the Tower Grove Baptist Church in St. Louis. His letter of January 25, 1960 revealed the deception of his previously taken stance of friendship.[5]

The pattern of many things to come, then and now, were contained in that letter. The letter was written long before the technical movement known as "church growth" was popularized by the organization based at Fuller Theological Seminary in California. Even then, however, it was obvious that, for Douglas and others, everything was judged by numbers and that bigness was the criterion for everything. Pressure for conformity was couched in terms of numerical and monetary clout. Faithfulness was determined by whether methods did or did not work. Those were the beginning

---

[4]Smith, *The Power Game* (New York: Random House, 1988).
[5]Douglas, letter to President Berquist, 25 January 1960, 2.

years of the super church. Theological integrity was a secondary consideration. It was likewise the day when any method was considered ethical, no matter how devious, if it accomplished the goal of orthodoxy. It was just a short time after Douglas's letter that it was discovered that for many months he had planted students in the classrooms. These students had been instructed to feed their classroom notes back to Douglas for his personal use, no matter what the context or the original purpose of the material. The power game, too frequently present in religious circles in recent years, was already operative. Less than two weeks following Douglas's letter, an invitation for me to speak at the St. Louis Pastors' Conference was cancelled. The blackballing had begun.

## 2. Trustee Committee Affirms Direction

Mack Douglas sent class notes compiled by some three students to a couple of other pastors in the St. Louis area. Letters were in turn addressed to the seminary, asking for the immediate dismissal of William Morton, professor of Archaeology, and me. In February 1960 it was necessary for us to have an all-day session with six of our trustees. At that time, we thought it to be one of the most significant meetings held on the campus of the young institution, and it appeared to set the direction for the future. President Berquist had told us the night before the meeting that he felt our perspective was his, or at least that he had confidence in our perspective, and that to question us was to question his leadership. He bravely took the lead in the meeting and indicated that we were building a seminary and not a Bible school. Two other professors were with us: Heber Peacock, professor of New Testament, and Morris Ashcraft, professor of theology. As the day concluded, the trustees pledged themselves to be one hundred percent behind us. Dr. H. I. Hester, chairman of the board of trustees and affiliated with nearby William Jewell College as professor of Old Testament, took me to lunch and reaffirmed the direction. He said he had been in Missouri for thirty years, understood the situation, and that had we not run into some difficulty already, he would have felt that we were reneging on our jobs.

This little trustee interlude is important because it indicates the official direction of the institution until the political tides later became more negative. When political tides change, it is amazing how quickly philosophical and theological positions become expendable. A few letters of affirmation were received from faculty members at other Southern Baptist institutions. As time passed and the outside political climate changed, security dictated caution, and former friends, at best, communicated no more; at worst, they joined those whom formerly they scorned. A lesson learned in philosophical and theological struggle is that one must count the risks involved, decide whether the cause or integrity dictate taking the risk, and then be willing to accept the consequences. Hard decision making cannot be done on the basis of supposed friendship support; in the thick of battle, one cannot depend on fair-weather "friends."

During this time, the book, *The Message of Genesis*, was being processed by Broadman Press. Broadman was aware of the static, but, reassured by Midwestern Seminary, agreed with the seminary that they had a mission to fulfill and some specific needs to meet. The future appeared to be very bright—in spite of the problems.

The atmosphere of encouragement continued, and it appeared that we were "over the hump" when my appointment to deliver a series of lectures to Missouri Baptist pastors at their summer conference at the Windermere Retreat Center was confirmed. Following the conference, Bruce C. Maples, the associate executive secretary of Missouri Baptists, sent me a letter requesting outlines for some four pastors, at which time he wrote:

> I don't think I ever enjoyed hearing Bible teaching any more than I did listening to you. I hope our students at Midwestern realize what a marvelous opportunity they have.[6]

A few days later, the pastor of the First Baptist Church, Jefferson City, Missouri, the city in which the Missouri Baptist headquarters was located, wrote:

> Let me thank you for filling in for me on Sunday while I was on vacation. So many of our people have expressed appreciation for your

---

[6]Maples, letter to the author, 7 September 1960.

messages and fine spirit. I heard the morning broadcast, as I had attended services down at the lake earlier, and am personally grateful for your splendid message. Our people have the feeling that Midwestern is in good hands.[7]

All this was most encouraging since it appeared to indicate that the official leadership in Missouri had not been gathered up in the campaign. Such accolades were short-lived, however, and ominous storm warnings were raised when Pastor Mack Douglas requested a personal meeting on December 5, 1960. The meeting was uneventful, but it soon became apparent that he was not a person to give up on his destructive project. Although letters of support had come from most of the staff of the Missouri Baptist Convention, including the executive secretary and the editor of the state Baptist newspaper *The Word and Way*, the atmosphere gradually changed as the pastor of one of the strongest financial church bases in the state kept up the pressure. Money talks—even in religious circles.

### 3. The Fateful Year

The new year 1961 began with Broadman's determination to publish the book. The galley proofs came while I was in the hospital for surgery and I corrected the galley proofs from the hospital bed so Joseph F. Green, general book editor, might have them in his hands by March 15. President Berquist was enthusiastic because it further undergirded the direction of the seminary. On April 24, 1961, Berquist wrote the following letter to William Fallis, editor, Broadman Press:

> I am pleased to learn that Broadman Press is in the process of publishing the manuscript of Dr. Ralph H. Elliott on the message of Genesis. I feel sure that many will agree with the statement from your office that this is one of the finest pieces of biblical scholarship produced by Southern Baptists since the days of Dr. A. T. Robinson and Dr. H. E. Dana.
>
> Here is to be found an honest, courageous, sincere endeavor to determine and present the meaning and message of this tremendously

---

[7]Thomas W. Nelson, letter to the author, 12 September 1960.

significant portion of Scripture. Dr. Elliott gives to Genesis an interpretation that reveals its message as highly relevant to the age in which we live. It is the work of a brilliant young scholar, who is also a devout and dedicated Christian. No one can read this book without feeling keenly the deep sense of holy reverence with which the author approaches his task and deals with his materials.

The author's knowledge and grasp of what has been written in this field is amazing. His ability to employ the tools of Hebrew linguistics, archaeology, and social history is strikingly impressive. He has rendered Southern Baptists and other Christian groups a genuine service in this scholarly yet profound spiritual treatment.[8]

In his enthusiasm President Berquist obviously overstated the case. Nevertheless, given the stress and strains of the time and the political risk to himself and to his institution, the letter was an act of moral courage and left no doubt about President Berquist's determined direction for the seminary. The direction was set and the die was cast. It looked momentarily as if things had been turned around. It appeared that even the severest critic had changed his mind, because Mack Douglas wrote on June 21, 1961,[9] requesting that I supply his pulpit for the two morning services and also the evening service on Sunday, September 17, 1961. It should be added, however, that the tide changed again and the invitation was withdrawn in an additional letter dated August 22, 1961.[10] Mack Douglas's vacillation may have been an indication that all the political teams were not yet in place and he was jockeying for position so as to be on the winning team, or the power broker for such, whatever it might happen to be.

*a. Early Noises.* The book was published in July, and immediately the campaign began again. The first shots in the new effort were fired by John F. Havlik, at that time director of Evangelism for Kansas Baptists. Havlik wrote three lengthy pieces, which were widely circulated. His articles were well written, and he initiated a line of attack that ultimately won many to the fundamentalist cause.

---

[8]Berquist, letter to William J. Fallis, 24 April 1961.
[9]Douglas, letter to the authhor, 21 June 1971.
[10]Douglas, letter to the author, 22 August 1961.

In his article "The Saviour and the Scriptures," Havlik developed the thesis that Jesus gave blanket approval to everything in the Old Testament and that to question any aspect of the Old Testament was to question the authority and the divinity of Jesus. Havlik expressed himself in a line of argument that we were to hear often:

> Our use of the word "critical" in regard to Old Testament scholarship is to denote those scholars who are not willing to accept the Lordship of Jesus Christ in regard to the Old Testament. That is, they are not willing to accept what he says and approach the Old Testament by substituting their own reason for His Lordship.[11]

Shortly after John Havlik's efforts, I was surprised to learn, through letters received, radio talks, rumors, and all sorts of ways, that I did not accept the classical statement of the divine-humanness of Jesus and that I was an unbeliever with regard to Jesus and the Christian gospel.

It was during those days that I learned how gullible much of the church community was and how ready to follow anything that was negative. It was also during that time that I recognized how dependent laity were upon the "preachers" or professional church leaders. The "priesthood-of-the-believer" aspect of Baptist tradition was not a reality, and it was very easy for clergy-types to violate their sacred trusts. It is amazing that some twenty-six years later at the meeting of the Southern Baptist Convention in San Antonio, June 14-16, 1988, the convention passed a resolution "On the Priesthood of the Believer." This so-called "Resolution No. 5" indicates that history, theology, and tradition can be bent to serve the will of power.

Havlik's efforts were joined by those of Earl L. Pounds, pastor of Mary Ann Baptist Church in St. Louis. Pounds was painstaking in writing an evaluation of *The Message of Genesis* which was circulated widely across the Southern Baptist Convention. I do not know who provided the funds for the venture, but the cost of circulating the

---

[11]Havlik, "The Saviour and the Scriptures," July 1961, 2. Havlik circulated this article widely by mail. One can only assume that the significant costs of such wide circulation came from Kansas Baptist evangelism and mission funds.

eleven-page document was no small amount.

Like Havlik, Pounds accused me of totally disregarding the New Testament which he interpreted from a literalist's point of view. Pounds also added something that had not appeared before. He excerpted material from Clyde T. Francisco's book *Introducing the Old Testament,* and used it to defend the Mosaic authorship of the Pentateuch. He referred to Francisco as my "teacher," and then indicated that I had betrayed both my teacher and Jesus.[12]

Whether Pounds rightly or wrongly used Francisco's material, from then on my former mentor and teacher was cast on the other side of the dispute. When Francisco addressed the St. Louis Pastors' Conference a short time later, he was greeted as a hero and appeared to give encouragement to the efforts of the St. Louis critics. Thus two aspects had been joined: a bridge had been formed between grassroots efforts in Kansas and Missouri, and a context had been created that placed the popular teacher over and against his former pupil.

Earl Pounds' efforts may have been sincerely motivated. Nevertheless, he used a technique that appears to be characteristic of many people from the "orthodox" camp who seek to defend their position by attacking another. That technique is to quote material that defends a position or alludes to a position that the one being attacked has not taken. The unsuspecting general reader neither knows that nor takes time to research the validity of the use of the material. The person on trial is guilty by implication. This was the case in the way Earl Pounds used Francisco's material. It is characteristic in the methodology of the literalist debates across the centuries.

*b. Possible Wider Implications.* Ever sensitive to the activities of its individual parts, the establishment in Nashville appears to have monitored events as they developed. Letters and communications were solicited by the self-appointed defenders of the faith, and people were encouraged to write to the offices of Broadman Press,

---

[12]Pounds, "The Message of Genesis, an Evaluation," July 1961, see esp. 9-10. Note once again that these "privately" circulated manuscripts were the main tool during the early days of the controversy.

to the offices of the Executive Committee of the Southern Baptist Convention, and to the people who might be influential in helping the so-called conservative (fundamentalist) cause.

As is ever the case—as it continues to be in the current Southern Baptist chaos—the literalists sought to divide people into conservatives and liberals. "Liberal" was and is, of course, a dirty word in the Southern Baptist context. Care was given to have it connote the old 1920s kind of theological liberalism. This certainly did not fit the situation then, nor does it fit the situation now. *The Message of Genesis* was quite conservative in its approach, "old shoe" for many biblical scholars. A member of another denomination read the work and said that he could readily understand the furor because it was "such a conservative book." He was speaking in jest, but it was an accurate statement of the case. It had a new look and may have appeared "liberal" to some Southern Baptists simply because denominational agencies had not published that kind of literature before. A "liberal," however, was anyone who did not agree with the defenders of orthodoxy. The word was knowingly used to connote antagonism and to attract camp followers.

The tactic was working, and the SBC Executive Committee began to take notice. Periodically, we received a tally from the Nashville offices as to how well the target mail was succeeding. I well remember the sad day when more letters "against" than "for" were reported and the spectre was raised that Cooperative Program receipts might be affected.

For non-Southern Baptist readers, the Cooperative Program is the name of the SBC scheme of united mission giving to and through the denomination. In the takeover struggle in the convention during the 1970s and 1980s, loyalty or disloyalty—the amount given or not given through the Cooperative Program—seemed to be as sacred, or more so, than any other issue, including that of the Bible. In the 1960s, the fundamentalists were the Cooperative Program loyalists. In the 1970s-1980s, the fundamentalists often were not strong Cooperative Program supporters. One of the charges brought against Charles Stanley, pastor of the First Baptist Church of Atlanta, upon his nomination by the right wing as a convention presidential candidate, was that he had not led his church to support the

Cooperative Program as it might have. There is continuing fallout and fragmentation with regard to the Cooperative Program issue. Both sides in the most recent Southern Baptist wars have proposed a variety of alternate methods for mission and program funding.

It may have been coincidence, but when reverberations were heard after the book's publication and when concern began to surface about Cooperative Program receipts, the Southern Baptist Convention Executive Committee requested each seminary president to prepare a position paper that would give a theological postulate for the existence of the institution. The request was sufficiently disturbing to Midwestern's president that he connected it with our immediate situation and passed a copy of the request to me for my appraisal.[13]

Two current connections come to mind. The first relates to the reading patterns of Southern Baptists, the other relates to the organizational structure of the Southern Baptist Convention. The publication arms of Southern Baptists have been so prolific and the skills at programming so superb that most Southern Baptists across the years have read literature produced largely in-house. As I recall from my own pregraduate school days at Southern Seminary, even pastors had only limited exposure to ecumenical publications. Unfamiliar with what was available, many Southern Baptists considered anything not encountered before as "liberal." To be so ingrown and inbred is terribly restrictive.

The other connection was equally relevant for the final determination of the Genesis issue. When the Southern Baptist Convention was organized in 1845, there were at least two choices available as organization styles. The "board style," was more centralized; the "societal style," was more tentative. Baptist life in the United States prior to 1845 had been conducted primarily through a pattern of societies. A society was organized for the support of some particular endeavor. Anyone who contributed to the society was a member of the society. Each society was independent. The Baptists who gathered in Augusta, Georgia in 1845 and organized the Southern

---

[13]Albert McClellan, program planning secretary, SBC Executive Committee, letter to President Berquist, 20 July 1961.

Baptist Convention utilized the board concept of organization. Although much denied, this gave an immediate centralization and has served the Southern Baptist Convention well as a source of organizational and programmatic strength, and has given a certain amount of centralized influence over its agencies. Southern Baptists speak much of the freedom of the individual, of the individual parts of the organization, and of the churches. Yet it is the more centralized of the two groups as compared with the loosely knit American Baptist Convention which was structured by the societal method. If not centralized in fact, the Southern Baptist Convention was and is centralized in patterns of persuasion and psychological influence.

Thus, there was ample cause for fear when the Southern Baptist Convention Executive Committee made its request for the composition of a "theological postulate." The wider implications were real, as was evidenced in the ultimate culmination in the vested and persuasive influence of the convention president, Dr. Herschel Hobbs, who was the final voice leading to Dr. Berquist's capitulation. As communions like the Presbyterians and Lutherans have discovered in the merger efforts of more recent years, the nature of one's polity and ecclesiastical organization can have far-reaching influence on the ultimate outcome of events.

*c. Activity on the State Level.* Initially, it appeared that storm clouds had appeared only in Missouri and Kansas. The weather was unsettled in Oklahoma, however, and it was not long until the weather patterns had connected. In August 1961, the Oklahoma County Pastors' Conference took the occasion of an address given by Professor Dale Moody of Southern Seminary as opportunity to pass a resolution that by implication included Midwestern Seminary and me.

Professor Moody had addressed a Bible conference at Shawnee, Oklahoma, at which he expressed himself concerning such things as "alien immersion" and the "security of the believer." He intimated that Oklahoma Baptists were "landmark Baptists" on these and other issues. Although it was Moody's presentation that served as the immediate catalyst, the pastors' conference used the occasion to include in its resolution an objection to a teacher in any of the seminaries being allowed to teach or write things they considered to cast doubt upon the authenticity of the word of God.

Oklahoma ultimately became one of the most antagonistic states, and this was the first of its many rumblings. Jack L. Gritz, editor of the *Baptist Messenger*, Oklahoma Baptist state paper, was especially venomous in his writings as he worked at keeping things "stirred up." The ferment contributed to the holding of a caucus meeting at Oklahoma City in March 1962, a meeting which had far-reaching significance, for it was in that meeting that the strategy for "take-over" was planned.

The resolution passed at that 1961 Oklahoma pastors' conference had immediate impact. So far as I can ascertain, the use of the resolution first appeared in local discussions with reference to Midwestern at a prayer service held in the Bethany Baptist Church of Kansas City shortly after the Oklahoma event. The Bethany Church considered the adoption of a similar resolution, but such did not materialize then. It is interesting, however, that at the time these deliberations were held at Bethany, the executive secretary of the Kansas Convention of Southern Baptists was in Kansas City and in conversation with the pastor of the Bethany Church. The linkages between persons in the various states were definitely in their formative stages.

In the midst of this atmosphere, I received two pieces of mail that indicated the plot was widening. One letter, dated August 22, 1961 and from Mack R. Douglas, cancelled a long-standing engagement at his church. The other was the first of many letters from Jack L. Gritz of the *Baptist Messenger*, in which he wrote:

> Frankly, I do not believe Southern Baptists are going to accept this sort of teaching in their seminaries. In fact, I am amazed that a Southern Baptist professor would say such things or write them for publication. I sincerely hope that you will turn away from such liberal thinking which has been the blight of other denominations.[14]

In spite of the bridging from state to state, the reality of denominational politics had not yet grasped either President Berquist or me. We were both quite naive about political processes, and assumed

---

[14]Gritz, letter to the author, 25 August 1961.

that all one needed to do in the faith community was to give accurate and rational response and truth would prevail. Eschatologically, the truth will prevail, but politics within religious circles and in the environs of ecclesiastical institutions causes truth-triumphant a long delay. To this day, I do not understand how it can be so lightly assumed that deviousness is a valid method in "defending the Gospel."

Not quite aware of the impact of Oklahoma Baptist politics, I sought to respond to what I thought was an earnest inquiry from Jack Gritz. Later, I learned that when there is an ambiguous mix of politics, power, and religion, rational response to an emotional expression is a useless enterprise. I share here something of my response so the general tenor of my own concerns might be grasped. My concern was in terms of preaching, the nature of biblical literature, and historicity.

As to preaching, I wrote:

> You will have noticed that my effort has been directed towards an appreciation for the message of this and other Old Testament books. Far too long this portion of the Bible has been ignored. I am concerned that it become again a portion of our preaching diet. I believe that God who inspired it initially wishes to use it over and over for continuing inspiration and revelation.[15]

With reference to the nature of literature, I sought to establish a common identity with the emphasis that was to be found in the other Southern Baptist seminaries at that time:

> As you have correctly assessed, I, like the Old Testament men in our other seminaries, recognize a difference of literary style between chapters 1-11 and 12-50, even as the parable of Jesus and the historical narration in the New Testament are of different literary style, yet devoted to the same inspired purpose of presenting God's revelation. The basic question is not whether the Hebrews did or did not use raw materials of other peoples. The emphasis is that the Hebrew writers wrote with a theological and religious purpose—that of magnifying the sole God as Creator, Lord, and Sustainer of nature and man. This was

---

[15]My letter to Gritz, 31 August 1961.

a witness which the ancient world had not known before. It was the pointing of the raw material towards a new and different understanding and purpose which showed it to be God-breathed and driven.[16]

I also called attention to the considerable attention I had given by way of digression in upholding the historicity of the patriarchs and of undergirding a religion that was historical and real. My personal theological frame of reference was indicated when I suggested:

> My views would not be accepted by liberalism and are not to be equated with theological liberalism. The theological interpretation of the Scripture which I advocate is a far cry from, as you express it, the "liberal thinking which has been the blight of other denominations."[17]

Such explanations were and are fruitless. Denominational functionaries are too often more interested in political and power aspects. Even Mr. Gritz had, in inference, suggested that my crime lay, at least partially, in "writing such things for publication." Most critics were aware that the views expressed were rather generally held in the Southern Baptist institutions. A great part of my crime was in the failure to doublespeak, thought to be so necessary in holding the loyalty of the constituency and in sustaining regularity in financial giving patterns. Institutional disease often causes us to be blind to our own motivations.

*d. Missouri Repercussions.* The flack raised by the Oklahoma event definitely added to the tension in Missouri. The clearest evidence was in a "command performance" before the Committee on Order of Business for the Missouri Baptist Convention. In January of 1961, I had been asked to give seven Bible studies, one each to introduce the seven sessions of the Missouri Baptist Convention, to be held in December of that year. However, the president of the convention, James Shirley, made it clear that if I were to appear on the program, he would probably refuse to preside. At Mr. Shirley's behest, the Committee on Order of Business insisted that I be present for a long interrogation as to my orthodoxy. The meeting began at 8:00 a.m. on a Saturday morning, September 9, 1961, in Jefferson

---

[16]Ibid.
[17]Ibid.

City, Missouri. I was presented with "certain charges" in order to allow the committee to determine my fitness to appear on the convention program. It was suggested that if I appeared on the program, my "presence would inject a disturbing element into the convention, perhaps even a floor fight involving Midwestern Seminary."[18]

During that meeting, it was mentioned that criticism was coming from Oklahoma City and from the Kansas Baptist offices in Wichita. The meeting was inconclusive and adjourned with plans to meet with Mr. Shirley on September 19. It was significant for me, and a clear signal was sent, when Midwestern's President Berquist, who had been summoned with me to the meeting, said as we neared adjournment, "I want you all to know that I will go along with Ralph Elliott all the way and I will be right at his side when the controversy arises."[19]

One totally new element did surface during the morning of the meeting with the Committee on Order of Business. It became obvious from the discussions in the meeting that Joseph McClain, who taught New Testament at Midwestern for a brief period and then went to a church pastorate, had helped to initiate the charges and was in regular contact with the Oklahoma, Kansas, and Missouri forces.

Prior to my meeting with Mr. Shirley on September 19, two Kansas City churches passed identical resolutions on September 13. The resolutions condemned me and the seminary and urged Broadman Press, the book-publishing arm of Southern Baptists, to "refrain from publishing such books which depart from our Southern Baptist position on the word of God." The two churches were Bethany and Beaumont Baptist Churches. With this added pressure, it was no surprise when I was removed from the Missouri Baptist Convention program at the September 19 meeting with Mr. Shirley.

One of the interesting questions at this time was where Earl

---

[18]From the minutes of the proceedings of the Program Committee of the Missouri Baptist Convention, 9 September 1961.
[19]Ibid.

Harding, the executive secretary of Missouri Baptists, stood in all of this. A trustee of Midwestern, Harding had been giving personal assurances to President Berquist and me that he was very supportive. In the September 19 meeting, however, his several comments were very inconclusive and appeared to be so phrased as to place him on the "winning side," whichever that might turn out to be. This ambiguous doublespeak disease proved to be insidious and appeared frequently. Initially, Harding kept all options open and the best evidence indicates that he was in conversation with all sides and was prepared to go in whichever direction gained the most momentum and support.

    *e. Initial Trustee Involvement.* At least, such impressed me as the case when the trustees of the seminary began to be pulled into the building storm. Earlier events led to a meeting of the executive committee of the seminary board of trustees on September 20, 1961. At that time, an investigating committee was appointed to hold a hearing to allow anyone who wished to present charges to do so. The committee was to report to the full board of trustees with recommendation for action.

    Earl Harding telephoned me following the September 20 meeting and asked for an appointment on October 2. At that meeting, his ostensible purpose was to placate me because of my removal from the program of the Missouri Baptist Convention. He said he regretted the necessity of my removal from the program, but that in these matters, it is necessary to do what one must in order to preserve peace. My sensitive antenna suggested that here was a person who would embrace whatever talisman might be necessary for survival. Before the meeting ended, the handwriting on the wall was very clear. I was shocked when he suggested that I write something which might indicate that what I had written in my book was not something strongly held, but a kind of "theory" that some might hold. I took the visit to be an indication of the strategy to come in the future, that is, that remarks be tailor-made according to circumstance so that anyone, of whatever persuasion, might feel supported. My notes also indicate that following the meeting, I wrote myself a memorandum, suggesting that Dr. Harding did not desire to put himself on record. He made it clear that he would not endanger himself with his Missouri Baptist constituents.

For me the most shocking discovery of the developing scenario was a growing realization, strongly and painfully painted in the October 2 meeting, that in religious circles integrity is a slippery commodity. Things were not generally evaluated by integrity, but by how well they would wear in the religious community. Window dressing was more important than substance. As will become clear at a later point, this was still Dr. Harding's concern at the very last trustee meeting when I was dismissed from the seminary. Is it any wonder that the phrase "preacher's talk" has come to be the nomenclature for things that may be more fantasy than fact? At any rate, by October 1961, only four months or less since the publication of *The Message of Genesis*, the Oklahoma, Kansas, and Missouri triangle had become a pressure to be reckoned with and people were running for cover. Trustees were on the spot.

It should be said, however, that the seven-man investigating committee and the board of trustees sought to perform their function during these early days in an honorable fashion. The investigating committee met for two full days, November 30 and December 1, 1961. One day was spent with me and another day was spent listening to the twenty-five to thirty-five pastors from Kansas and Missouri who firmly pressed for my dismissal. The committee summarized its findings under two main points: (1) the nature of the biblical revelation and (2) the nature of theological education. The writings of E. Y. Mullins and W. T. Connor, names respected by all factions, revered former professors at Southern and Southwestern seminaries, respectively, were cited to support the validity of the approach taken, not only in the book under question but also in Midwestern Seminary generally.[20]

The trustees' investigating committee felt that the heart of the question it faced was the purpose of theological education. While the

---

[20]Cf., e.g., E. Y. Mullins, *The Christian Religion in Its Doctrinal Expression* (Nashville: The Sunday School Board of the Southern Baptist Convention, 1917; often reprinted, notably by American Baptist's Judson Press) and W. T. Conner, *Revelation and God: An Introduction to Christian Doctrine* (Nashville: Broadman Press, 1936).

committee indicated the necessity of the minister giving attention to the sermonic and devotional treatment of the Scriptures, it stressed the necessity of basing such a treatment upon an understanding of the nature of the Scriptures, the nature of its authority, and the nature of its message. The committee's report ended with the following affirmation:

> We take pride in the scholarship, theological and denominational soundness, and evangelistic witness of the institution.[21]

The full board met in a special session to consider the matter on December 28-29, 1961. The results were most gratifying to me personally. The board noted that there were honest differences of opinion and released a resolution with the following affirmation:

> BE IT THEREFORE RESOLVED that while there are members of the board of trustees who are in disagreement with some of the interpretations presented by Dr. Elliott in his book, we do affirm our confidence in him as a consecrated Christian and a promising scholar and teacher, a loyal servant of Southern Baptists, and a dedicated and warmly evangelistic preacher of the Gospel.[22]

Some of the input in that meeting was more significant than the resolution itself. The trustees made an honest effort to probe the nature of the biblical revelation. It is important to note that here because the discussion then was so similar to the most recent debates among Southern Baptists. It is further evidence that the various strands of the Southern Baptist heritage have always been fragilely united. The following was used by the special committee in making its presentation to the board:

> Baptists do not demand nor have they ever demanded a uniformity of belief about the method of inspiration. To attempt to do so now would be a denial of our basic position as Baptists and a tragic infidelity to our heritage. Undoubtedly, there are those who, like the group demanding Dr. Elliott's dismissal, would contend for biblical literalism as the only

---

[21]"Special Committee—Board of Trustees," the investigating committee's report, 1 December 1961, 3.
[22]"Midwestern Trustee Resolution," 28 December 1961.

true view of inspiration. But it should never be forgotten that there are also vast numbers of Southern Baptists who do not believe in the plenary verbal theory.[23]

The issues of today were the issues then. Although there were certainly elements of a power struggle, which were and were not related to the theological issues involved, that board of trustees demonstrated both sophistication and integrity in trying to address the crisis at hand. They demonstrated an awareness that the context was larger than Midwestern Seminary and had implications for the entire denomination. The board also demonstrated considerable courage.

It was a naive to assume, however, that this singular decisiveness would stop the critics. Furthermore, Midwestern, a relatively new institution, was viewed as competition by Southern, the mother seminary of them all. Midwestern, therefore, was standing alone. Seminary educators and administrators elsewhere in Southern Baptist life had yet to grasp that one institution's plight was ultimately the plight of them all.

## 4. The Wider Implications

The convergence of forces from Missouri, Kansas, and Oklahoma suggested even prior to the December 1961 trustees meeting that there were much larger implications both politically and theologically. Pressure was already being applied to the Sunday School Board and Broadman Press. It was widely reported that as early as August 1961, some Broadman Book Store managers had received such pressure that they had removed the book from their shelves and that it took a private request to uncover its availability for purchase. When this rumor was brought to the attention of Broadman Press, the general book editor reported that "each book store manager is responsible for what he stocks and how he displays."[24] Jay O. Turner, manager of the Book Store Department, Merchandise and

---

[23]Cf. Sally Rice, "Ralph Elliott: Controversial Figure among Southern Baptists," a paper presented to the Duke University Department of Religion (15 April 1963) 26.

[24]Joseph F. Green, Jr., letter to the author, 18 September 1961.

Sales Division of the Sunday School Board, indicated a general policy of openness and made it clear that "we have no fear about displaying or selling *The Message of Genesis.*"[25]

By December 1961, the Sunday School Board, parent body of Broadman Press, was receiving heavy criticism. The board traditionally had a Home Week each December when every employee was expected to cancel any engagements in the field and to participate in various Home Week functions. *The Message of Genesis* was an issue for discussion during the 1961 Home Week. Shortly thereafter, James L. Sullivan, executive secretary-treasurer of the board, indicated that "although he did not agree with everything in the book, we had an obligation as a publishing house in its behalf as a textbook."[26]

During the exchanges regarding Sunday School Board activities, I learned that originally the decision to publish the book had been made at the top echelons of management. Furthermore, the decision was made only after an exchange of correspondence between Dr. Sullivan of the Sunday School Board and President Berquist of Midwestern Seminary. Joseph Green indicated that "Dr. Berquist's statement was the final factor that influenced our decision to publish, but I am sure that Dr. Sullivan has never said that it was the only factor."[27]

The general perception and reaction of the Sunday School Board at the time may be gleaned from its statement of position as adopted by the fifty-four-member board at its semiannual meeting, January 29-31, 1962. Although the statement from the board is long, it must be seen in its entirety to grasp the strength of the board at that particular time. The statement suggests the board perceived that in broad terms across the denomination an age of maturity had come. In light of later events, a reading of the statement can only cause one to ask "What happened?" Here is what the Sunday School Board said:

> In 1898, the Southern Baptist Convention authorized the board to

---

[25]Turner, letter to the author, 18 September 1961.

[26]This word was included in a letter from William J. Fallis to the author, 7 December 1961.

[27]Green, letter to the author, 26 January 1962.

publish books. This assignment was reaffirmed at least six times in the subsequent 25 years. In 1934, the board began to use the Broadman Press as its imprint for general books. Throughout the book publishing history of the Sunday School Board, there has not been the slightest doubt of its serious and significant responsibility in general book publishing.

The Southern Baptist Convention gave further clarification when in 1959 it adopted a resolution which stated, "All agencies of the convention should continue to utilize the services of the Sunday School Board to the maximum feasible extent for editing, printed materials, filming, filmstrips, recordings and other materials that are to be sold."

*Manuscript Evaluation*

Thus established by convention action as publishing house for the denomination, and with distinctive objectives stated, the Sunday School Board, through its Broadman Books Department, evaluates hundreds of manuscripts each year. In the course of such evaluation, the manuscript of *The Message of Genesis* was presented with the thought that the book be published by Broadman Press for use as resource material for seminary students and for biblical study-in-depth by individuals.

In accepting the book for publication, Broadman Press recognized that the point of view expressed in the book would not be coincident with the thinking of all Baptists. It was considered, however, to be representative of a segment of Southern Baptist life and thought. Different viewpoints on the book of Genesis, and on other books of the Bible, have been published by Broadman Press. As a matter of fact, in carrying out its assignment, Broadman Press has approached such controversial subjects as the millennial question. It has published three books on this subject, all with differing points of view.

Broadman Press ministers to the denomination in keeping with the historic Baptist principle of the freedom of the individual to interpret the Bible for himself, to hold a particular theory of inspiration of the Bible which seems most reasonable to him, and to develop his beliefs in accordance with his theory.

The elected Sunday School Board hereby reaffirms its approval of the principles and policies under which Broadman Press is functioning, especially the objectives which are:

To publish books of Christian content and purpose:

1. For use in training ministers and other church leaders (including

textbooks for colleges and seminaries).

2. To assist churches in their worship, proclamation, education, and ministry.

3. To help persons in the area of personal faith, personality development, character growth, and human relations.

4. To be representative of Southern Baptist life and thought.

5. For all ages in such classifications as Bible study, Christian biography and fiction, devotional experiences, inspiration, evangelism, doctrine, stewardship, missions and life situations.

The elected Sunday School Board further encourages Broadman Press to continue to publish books which will present more than one point of view, and which will undergird the faith and contribute to the Christian growth and development of those who read them.[28]

The avowed purpose of the board was to publish materials representative of various segments of Southern Baptist life and thought (number 4 above). *The Message of Genesis* met both that criterion and the board's desire to publish material which might be used for college and seminary textbooks. Unfortunately, the seminaries and other educational institutions appeared by either default or design to want to hide the fact that they at times represented various points of view, and sought to avoid any suspicion that they were at variance with any part of the constituency. The Sunday School Board's statement, although defensive, was a strong one and deserved more support and affirmation than it received from the educational institutions. For that reason, the educational institutions must be charged, at least in part, for the right-wing chaos in which the Southern Baptist Convention finds itself today. The seminaries, in particular, were guilty of a failed stewardship.

At the same time, the Sunday School Board policy was broad enough to provide an umbrella for the publishing of a one-perspective conservative commentary such as is currently in process. Statements by elected Southern Baptist leaders during the decades of the 1970s and 1980s will indicate, however, that such latitude will no longer be allowed. The leadership cadre of the 1980s, and now the 1990s, has made it quite clear there is a particular theological test

---

[28]Baptist Sunday School Board *Newsletter* 6/3 (March 1962).

and that the test is firmly set in one direction. There has definitely been a disintegration of the wider freedom of earlier days. Old friends from seminary days and employees of the Sunday School Board for many years confide to me at the annual Baptist World Alliance Commission and Council meetings that each morning when they report to work, they do not know how much, if any, freedom they will have for that particular day's task. The right-wing authorities assume that survival depends upon countermodernization.

At any rate, one will have noted the broad base of support for publishing *The Message of Genesis,* including the public support of the Sunday School Board itself. Unfortunately, the scenario ultimately proved to be duplicitous: eventually the Sunday School Board succumbed to political pressure and withdrew from its commitment. Great fear seized the board. The development of the story must be delayed, but the board at a later date even claimed it had lost or inadvertently melted the plates of the book, evidently to avert any responsibility or criticism should it be reprinted by another publisher. When threatened with legal action, the board reported mysteriously finding the plates and somehow redeeming them from the smelter.

The Sunday School Board jumped ship. Indeed, when the seas were at their stormy heights, everyone deserted the ship and the author was in the boat alone. This is not such a bad plight, however, for thereby one learns things that can be learned nowhere else.

Ministry of any kind involves risks. In later years I have said to students and colleagues everywhere that one should count the risks to see whether they are important enough to take. Not every risk is so important. One should count the cost of the risk contemplated. Once the risk and the cost have been determined to be demanded by integrity, one goes ahead. Such a calculated decision does not allow me to cry "foul" when the risk has been taken, nor does it provide one leeway to feel sorry for oneself when the price is demanded. If one advocates taking up a cross, one has no grounds for crying because the cross is heavy.

*a. Antagonists Continue.* After the meeting of Midwestern Seminary's board of trustees in December 1961, and prior to the

January meeting of the Sunday School Board, strife was fueled with more anger. Some persons in the Midwest did not give a good reception to the positive affirmation from the board of trustees. Jack L. Gritz, editor of the Oklahoma *Baptist Messenger*, proclaimed that the supportive resolution by the board "was a tragic mistake," and that "any man who believes and teaches as does Professor Elliott has no place on the faculty of a Southern Baptist seminary." Gritz suggested something that proved to be very prophetic. Although, as mentioned previously, Judge Paul Pressler has been widely credited with the strategy of replacing disliked trustees with "safe" ones, Editor Gritz suggested that in Southern Baptist institutions the final voice resides with the convention and not the trustees and that the convention has the power to replace trustees as deemed necessary. He deemed it necessary and suggested that "such action must be taken."[29] Ultimately his suggestion was followed.

I carried a rather heavy agenda of speaking engagements while at Midwestern, and the wider implications of the controversy were evident in a rash of cancellations. They came in rapid succession from the Missouri Baptist Convention, the Missouri Evangelistic Conference, Hannibal-LaGrange College, Swope Park Baptist Church in Kansas City, the Harmony Baptist Association of Sedalia, Missouri, and so forth. The reasons for cancellation were numerous. Some were humorous. The pastor of the Swope Park Baptist Church in Kansas City (a trustee who later had an active part in my demise) indicated he would stay and preach himself on the Sunday I had been scheduled to speak so he could rest up two more days after surgery so as to be in better shape to go hunting. Others "told it like it was." Upon cancelling my engagement to give a series of lectures there, the president of Hannibal-LaGrange College wrote:

> I regret this more than I can say, but I am hesitant to hazard the involvement of Hannibal-LaGrange in a contention which seems to have grown quite sharp.[30]

The people in Sedalia, Missouri laid it on the line:

---

[29]Gritz, "Mistake at Midwestern," *Baptist Messenger,* 24 May 1962.
[30]President L. A. Foster, letter to the author, 3 October 1961.

In light of the feeling of some of our superintendents of missions and pastors, I feel it would be best to withdraw our invitation to you to come to teach STUDIES IN JEREMIAH for us at this time. Since this is a united effort on the part of several associations, some of the men would not participate if you came.[31]

Mack R. Douglas of Tower Grove Baptist Church in St. Louis aided the cause by circulating a mimeographed list of twenty heresies which some of my students had gleaned from their Old Testament Survey course under my instruction.

In spite of the support from the Midwestern trustees, hindsight suggests that the shaping of the coffin for the burial of my professorship began with one event that preceded both the meeting of the full board of seminary trustees and the meeting of the Sunday School Board and another event that followed those meetings. I refer to a widely circulated article by K. Owen White, "Death in the Pot," and to the caucus of interested parties in Oklahoma City in March 1962.

(1) "Death in the Pot." On October 26, 1961, Dr. K. Owen White, pastor of the First Baptist Church of Houston, Texas, sent an article entitled "Death in the Pot," based on 2 Kings 4:40, to all Baptist state papers, to the seminary presidents, to the Sunday School Board, and to many other leaders. Dr. White carried considerable political weight as the pastor of Houston's First Baptist Church and as chairman of the executive board of the Baptist General Convention of Texas. The article was cleverly done and well written. It was published widely and attracted much attention far and near. White took some eleven quotations from *The Message of Genesis* and underlined certain parts so as to highlight those words and phrases which, placed seriatim and without any context, made it appear that the author of such had no appreciation of the Bible. By White's own admission, he recognized that his method was less than fair, for he said:

I have made no attempt to review the book. The quotations speak for themselves. I have merely emphasized certain words and phrases in

---

[31]Sherman D. Bridgman, letter to the author, 1 November 1961.

these quotations to shed light upon the particular doctrinal or historical truth in question.[32]

White called the book "liberalism, pure and simple," suggested that it was poison, and that it would lead to "ultimate disintegration as a great New Testament denomination."[33] That is quite an indictment! The denomination of which he spoke is falling apart, but not because of a simple commentary on Genesis. It is being pulled apart and torn into shreds by those who have purported to be its saviors.

It was never my privilege to meet K. Owen White, but I had the impression in those days that his motivation was that of genuine concern. I did not have the impression that he was "power grabbing" as so often appeared to be true of the nucleus of critics in Missouri and Oklahoma. Nevertheless, White's words exploded like a bombshell, and the Missouri people skillfully used the article as a weapon. He was soon included in the Missouri-Oklahoma group as a strategizer and became the group's spokesperson at the meeting of the Southern Baptist Convention in San Francisco in June 1962. Dr. White became the spokesperson for conservatism and on that basis was elevated to the presidency of the Southern Baptist Convention.

**(2) The Oklahoma Caucus.** A matter closely related to "Death in the Pot," and perhaps energized by the attention the article received, was a meeting held in Oklahoma City, March 8-9, 1962. This meeting became the prototype for the kind of strategizing that captured control of the Southern Baptist Convention some twenty-five years later.

Some fifty people met at the Capitol Baptist Church in Oklahoma City, allegedly "to discuss the current theological crisis within the convention."[34] Various people attended the Oklahoma meeting: a lay person, denominational functionaries, and pastors. In the light of

---

[32]White, "Death in the Pot," 26 October 1961, 4.

[33]Ibid.

[34]This was the report in *The Baptist Standard,* the Baptist newspaper in Texas, 21 March 1962. The report was based on a news release by Jack Gritz of Oklahoma.

previous and future involvements, the active leadership participants were W. Ross Edwards, pastor of Swope Park Baptist Church in Kansas City and secretary of the Midwestern trustees; Mack R. Douglas, pastor of Tower Grove Baptist Church, St. Louis and a member of the Sunday School Board; Jack Gritz, editor of Oklahoma's *Baptist Messenger;* M. E. Ramsey of Oklahoma, the editor of an independent Baptist paper called *The Baptist Clarion;* and K. Owen White, author of "Death in the Pot." The widely represented group included people from Texas, Arkansas, Kansas, New Mexico, Colorado, Oklahoma, Tennessee, and Missouri.

Ross Edwards of Kansas City presented a keynote address in which he described the liberalism in the seminaries and warned that conservative Christians in Southern Baptist life would soon be in the minority unless definite action was taken. It was a gloom-and-doom speech in which he suggested that those not agreeing with the group failed to believe in the word of God and thereby would consign a denomination which had a glorious past to a very dark future. The group was urged to "stand together and wage a relentless battle for conservatism." His ringing challenge was that "the time has arrived for us to plan a strong defense against the threat of frigid intellectualism and liberalism which lead to destruction. May we, therefore, plan wisely, and well."[35] That was quite a statement from one who previously had commended me when I preached in his church as a "warm evangelical preacher," and who a few months earlier in a letter cancelling another preaching engagement in his church had signed his letter, "Always your friend."[36] This was, however, quite indicative of how relationships were, especially with the Missouri threesome of Ross Edwards, Earl Harding, and Mack Douglas. By telephone and in person they generally professed great friendship and admiration and concern for my well-being, but inevitably such professions of concern were followed by some kind of attack here or there. On an individual basis, these three found it difficult to deal

---

[35]Edwards, "Introductory Statement," Oklahoma City, 8 March 1962, as reported by Sally Rice in "Ralph Elliott: Controversial Figure among Southern Baptists" (see n. 23 above).

[36]Edwards, letter to the author, 11 October 1961.

with the issues as I assume they thought them to be. As the old saying goes, "With friends like that, who needs enemies?"

Edwards struck fire in his address. Particular attention was given to *The Message of Genesis* and threats were made that if something were not done, people in the heart of the convention would withdraw their churches. Even in those days, the affirmation of a literalistic and inerrantist approach to Scripture and an autocratic style of pastoral leadership appeared together. It was this mentality that years later culminated in "Resolution No. 5" of the Southern Baptist Convention, meeting in San Antonio, June 1988, in which it was indicated that the "Priesthood of the Believer" was to be interpreted as placing local authority in the hands of the pastor.

In his address to the caucus, Edwards called for a decision, and something was done. The group appealed to the Southern Baptist Committee on Committees and requested that conservative men be placed on the boards of the schools. By innuendo the group suggested that failure to do so might result in the presentation of a conservative slate to oppose that of the Committee on Committees at San Francisco when the annual meeting was held in June. According to various reports about the Oklahoma meeting, its major purpose and most immediate objective was "to secure the election for what the group considers theologically conservative men to the trustees of the Kansas Seminary."[37] Here again is evidence that the so-called "Pressler plan" for a ten-year takeover of the Southern Baptist Convention was born many years earlier. Another action of the Oklahoma City group was to raise funds to help finance an independent paper, *The Baptist Clarion,* so that it could be used to inform convention pastors of the "real issues." The *Clarion* was never of great significance, but it did serve as an early indication that the fragmentation of the convention for personal interest was never considered improper or unethical.

Planning power and grandstanding piety inevitably are twins. The caucus reported about itself that "the meeting was bathed with a spirit of humility and concern over resolving the difficulties within

---

[37]"Oklahoma City Group Weighs 'Current Crisis'," *The Arkansas Baptist Newsmagazine* 61 (22 March 1962) 3.

the denomination's organizational framework." It closed, according to the report, with these men "on their knees in prayer of dedication."[38]

Some state Baptist editors questioned the group's power and its piety. Such evaluations were made by both foe and friend of the group's theological position. Erwin L. McDonald of Arkansas was prophetic when he inquired:

> Have Southern Baptists come to the day when their affairs must be directed by rump sessions? If so, we have fallen on dark days. Something of far greater impact than the orthodoxy of seminary professors is involved here. For Baptists have never been a people to conduct their business any way but democratically and aboveboard. Surely we do not need anything that might remotely resemble a spiritual version of the Ku Klux Klan.[39]

James F. Cole of Louisiana, quite close to the basic sentiments of the group, accused its members of "dirty pool" and "stacking the deck"—great religious language—while suggesting:

> Their opposition is genuinely sincere, but are using it as a hobby horse to ride into the floor of the convention with the hope that they will come out king pins.
>
> I, for one, reject the form of liberalism which would destroy the New Testament doctrines, but by the same token, I refuse to be a card-carrying member of the society of authoritative dogmatism, for both constitute equal dangers to Baptists or any denomination.[40]

The comments of Cole were perceptive. He was dealing with both motivation and outcome. As to motivation, he was able to analyze some of the latent disappointment of at least one of the men present, Ross Edwards, when his offer to "serve the new seminary [Midwestern] in any way from janitor to president" did not catapult

---

[38]"Oklahoma City Group Weighs `Current Crisis'," Baptist Press release, 16 March 1962.

[39]McDonald, "More than Orthodoxy," *Arkansas Baptist Newsmagazine* 61 (22 March 1962) 4.

[40]Cole, "A Word of Caution," *The Baptist Message* 79 (15 March 1962) 2.

him into an administrative position. As to outcome, Cole recognized that such efforts as those by the people meeting in Oklahoma City would lead the convention away from a centrist position, which had been the binding and uniting power of the diverse elements constituting Southern Baptist life. The latter part of Cole's concern has been realized in the tragic and unseemly chaos of a Baptist people who have aborted their past and perhaps denied their better future.

Shortly after the reports of the Oklahoma meeting were circulated, one of my former students, recently graduated from Midwestern and in his first post-seminary pastorate, wrote a letter to President Berquist and me in which he shared words from somewhere in the writings of Samuel Coleridge:

> He, who begins loving Christianity better than Truth, will proceed by loving his own sect or church better than Christianity, and end in loving himself better than all.[41]

However one may have evaluated the Oklahoma meeting at that time, it appears obvious now that it was the watershed turning point in the steadily increasing crescendo.

*b. A Reflective Interlude.* I must confess I was hurting at this particular point. The hurt did not come from the critics but from uncertainty about my friends. For reasons I do not fully understand, I did not find the attacks about the book or about my viewpoints to be crushing. Generally, I felt more sympathy and compassion for the people who lashed out in such strong ways. There was little real anger. Seldom was there any bitterness, and there was almost no residual bitterness even when the matter was, so they thought, brought to a close with my dismissal from Midwestern Seminary. Across the years, I have reflected on the question of my concern and sympathy for the antagonists, rather than some other emotions. I think it perhaps relates to the fact that my own roots and my earlier religious mind-set were so close to theirs. I had made the transition from my own dogmatist-literalist beginnings and realized how difficult and how painful that growth process is. I understood

---

[41]Bill Nichols, letter to Berquist, 22 March 1962.

exactly where they were. I had been there. I retained some sense of appreciation and admiration for some of the values and for part of the value system they represented.

The discomfort I experienced related to friends and colleagues. It was not my nature in those days to form very many close professional relationships. I was rather young and so new to the field of teaching that there was much professional timidity on my part. I was still earning credibility, and I held a wholesome respect for those who were older and more experienced than I. There were two relationships that were most dear to me. The first was my love and appreciation for Southern Baptist Theological Seminary.

Although I felt compelled to pursue the opportunities at Midwestern, Southern was a kind of "Jerusalem" for me. Quite some time before the "Genesis controversy" became so intense, I had been asked to write an article for *The Review and Expositor,* the journal published by the Southern Seminary faculty. That request brought great joy to me because it was from the school and the faculty which I felt had given me some comprehension of growth and maturity.

However, as the controversy developed, word came now and then that the school was in various ways seeking to distance itself. I refused to believe such rumors but they appeared to be confirmed when *The Tie,* the seminary's quarterly newsmagazine, in the February 1962 issue had a listing of those who had written material for the particular issue of *The Review and Expositor* which was being advertised. My article was in that *The Review and Expositor,* but my name was the only author's name omitted from the promotion material in *The Tie.* It is, of course, possible this happened because of some oversight and may not have been intentional. In my frame of mind at the time, however, it was a confirmation of the rumors that I had heard and it caused great pain. It was clear to me that my school was disowning me. This understanding was encouraged by letters I received from two Southern faculty members at the time. The letters were strong denunciations of the omission. One of the letters suggested that my major professor had something to do with the omission; the second letter suggested that the administration had something to do with it. I concluded that both were correct and I felt great stress in being cut off from the institution I loved so much.

Time has proved that I was cut off. Prior to that time, I had received much attention from Southern and was regarded with popular affirmation. Since that time, there has been no openness to me, either officially or unofficially. I did visit the campus once following my dismissal and visited with students in a classroom. In effect, however, I was cut off. This was more painful to me than even my dismissal from the faculty at Midwestern.

As a matter of fact, Midwestern Seminary has demonstrated far more courage than Southern. Some years ago when my former colleague William T. Morton retired at Midwestern, I was invited to the retirement festivities, and President Milton Ferguson was a most gracious host and invited me to his office for lengthy conversation. The point is the school that taught me the rudiments of what I knew in the biblical field turned its back because it did not wish to lose popular favor through any identity with my Genesis struggles. There was a loneliness and a void in my being.

This has remained with me across the years. I have been conscious of having no theological school as an alma mater. Perhaps I did not myself realize how important this was to me until 1989. At the time, I was serving as the provost of the Colgate Rochester Divinity School. In the 1989 spring convocation, I was presented with a certificate naming me an honorary alumnus of the Colgate Rochester Divinity School. It was a simple thing and somewhat perfunctory, but I was amazed at the great swell of emotion that seized me in the realization that there was a school that wanted to claim me. Obviously something deep within me had been unattended for a long time.

Closely related to the institutional matter was the second relationship, that with my mentor and friend Clyde T. Francisco, my major professor at Southern. I have indicated elsewhere that Dr. Francisco was not at all happy with my election to the faculty at Midwestern, and he was even more unhappy at the small role I played in helping to bring dismissed Southern professors to the Midwestern faculty. Nevertheless, Francisco and I remained personal friends. There was a time when pleasing him and receiving his affirmation was regarded by me as of great importance.

Although I had not personally known Dr. Francisco prior to becoming a student at Southern, we were from the same city in Virginia, and I had read much about him in our local newspapers. He was something of a local hero, both because of his exploits as a football player and because of his academic achievements and his highly regarded professorship at Southern Seminary. He took an interest in me from the very beginning, and I feel rather certain that I would never have been elected to Southern's faculty without his sponsorship. It was he who insisted I give particular attention to the critical study of Genesis. I admired him very much.

I began agonizing over the apparent ambiguity and uncertainty in the relationship with Dr. Francisco as early as August-September 1961. It was the ambiguity that caused me pain, an ambiguity I was never able to comprehend. At some points, Dr. Francisco was highly complimentary and appeared to want to be supportive. Although Francisco made it clear from the very beginning that he disagreed with some of my conclusions, he, for instance, wrote to William Fallis of Broadman Press:

> Thank you for sending Ralph Elliott's *The Message of Genesis* to me. It is a book that gathers together in a most useful way the results of the extensive research now being done in Genesis. We will find it invaluable in my classes at the seminary, particularly in my course on Genesis where we will use it as a text.[42]

He thanked Broadman for having published the book and concluded with the comment that he wished I had shown more sensitivity to what he called the "cultural lag" of Southern Baptists.

Francisco's personal letters to me, with few exceptions, were always appreciative and at times critical of the critics. Along the way he was supportive through personal letters. When K. Owen White of Texas circulated his article "Death in the Pot," I responded with an interpretative piece that appeared in a number of various state Baptist papers. On that occasion, Francisco wrote to me as follows:

---

[42]Francisco, letter to Fallis with copy to the author, 5 October 1961.

Dear Ralph,

I have just read your defense in the *Biblical Recorder*. It is well done. You have many friends out there, including me.

It is too bad that men like K. O. White get frightened and bark at the wrong person. We are really confused when we can't tell our friends from our enemies! I guess you realize now how wide the gulf is between the latest scholarship and much of Texas. Let's hope it is not universal.

As ever,    *Clyde*[43]

While this letter was supportive, it was at the same time a chastisement. It continued a theme he had hammered home to me many times and over which we had a basic difference, that is, how much should we "let the people know," and the ability to speak in such a way (doublespeak) that you "knew what you knew" but which would not reveal to lay people what they did not want to know or what they could not or should not know. The theme had appeared in an earlier letter when he wrote:

> You have spoken into a theological vacuum, and your use of the liberal vocabulary conceals from them the fact that you are essentially a conservative and anything but a modernist. *They cannot understand you.*[44]

Our running debate regarding concealment and doublespeak continued for many years. During my years in Chicago, Francisco traveled to that region for numerous engagements. We would arrange to meet someplace, and the conversation and the disagreement were always the same. We engaged in that conversation even until his untimely death.

Most recently, when reading of the ongoing debate and struggle between Cardinal Joseph Ratzinger, prefect of the Sacred Heart Organization for the Doctrine of Faith in the Roman Catholic Church, and the Brazilian liberationist theologian Leonardo Boff, I had some new insights as to what was happening. Ratzinger had

---

[43]Francisco, letter to the author, 6 Febuary 1962.
[44]Francisco, letter to the author, 5 October 1961.

been Boff's teacher, but their journeys had taken them in different directions and into different sociological and political settings. They had some of the same concerns for the well-being of the church but had concluded that the interest of the church could best be served in two different ways. As the guardian of orthodoxy, Ratzinger became Boff's judge and believed that centralization within the mother institution was the only way of preserving and protecting the faith. Leonardo Boff viewed life from the underside in Brazil and came to understand the initiation of life and thought within the lay, base communities as the only way of protecting a meaningful and vibrant faith. It became a debate between control and freedom, the right to know and the right not to know.[45]

This is essentially the debate that has been taking place within the Southern Baptist Convention during the decades of the 1970s and 1980s as evidenced in a resolution previously mentioned, which essentially undergirded the pastor (priest) as being the one who should determine what Southern Baptist lay people should believe and do.[46] It is a continuation of the "Strange Bedfellows" theme, which I wrote in 1973 when I compared the centralization and dogmatism of Southern Baptists with the pre-Vatican II mentality of the Roman Catholic Church.[47] In a sense, it was a variation of the long-standing debate about the *magisterium*, the teaching office of the church. Martin Luther and John Calvin struggled with the issue and it continues to be at the heart of many problems in the Roman church today.[48]

Dr. Francisco contended it was because I could not communicate that I got into trouble; I contended it was because I deliberately *did* communicate that I got into trouble. Although I am sure he viewed the matter from the genuine concern to "protect the institution," I saw it as a matter of truth. Institutional preservation and truth

---

[45]See the excellent treatment by Harvey Cox, *The Silencing of Leonardo Boff* (Oak Park IL: Meyer Stone Books, 1988).

[46]"Resolution No. 5," *SBC Bulletin* 65 (15 June 1988) 6.

[47]Elliott, "Strange Bedfellows," in Claude A. Frazier, ed., *Shall Preachers Play God?* (Independence MO: Independence Press, 1973).

[48]See an excellent treatment of the "Magisterium" in Richard Osmer, *A Teachable Spirit* (Louisville: Westminster/John Knox Press, 1990) 73-135.

preservation have often been in conflict in the life of the church.

If there is a vacuum of understanding among lay members of the Southern Baptist Convention (or any other denomination), it is perhaps due to the failure of those who have neglected or avoided the opportunity across the years to share the kind of knowledge and experience that can help persons stretch, mature, and grow. Many things lead me to believe that lay people are far more capable of mature theological reflection and growth, openness, and acceptance than clergy-types would admit. Lay people are far more intuitive than professional clergy would give them credit for. Lay people do grapple with basic existential questions, although at times they are reluctant to express themselves because they might not have the ring of orthodoxy in terms acceptable to the clergy-types.

During the days of the so-called "Genesis controversy," I received enough correspondence to fill many file drawers. In recent years, I have managed to separate the clergy and lay letters and arrange them in different categories. The larger number of letters from clergy-types are negative, ugly, extremely critical, and even sexually suggestive. Quite the contrary, the lay correspondence is for the most part appreciative and supportive. One lady in Oklahoma wrote, for instance, that she wished someone had helped her family grapple with the nature of biblical revelation years earlier. Had someone done so, she believes, she would not have lost her four daughters' interest in the church. (The warmth of this kind of response has stayed with me for a long time.)

In my brief career as a divinity school academic officer, I have been involved in a project with church consultation among diverse denominations in different regions of the country. After each Friday-Sunday session, I have returned to the divinity school with the realization that lay theological education must be placed high on the list of priorities. Lay leaders have asked repeatedly for the same kind of theological reflection made available to seminaries. Many wish to participate in seminary courses with no difference in offering for the ordained and the nonordained. My experiences in recent years have confirmed my earlier conclusion that it is a sad mistake to assume the necessity of hiding one's best thought.

To pick up an earlier thread, my anguish in those days was not simply the difference in approach on the part of teacher and pupil. The pain came from the conflicting readings that came at different times and on different occasions. As he proffered me friendship and support, Dr. Francisco was a frequent and popular speaker before pastors' conferences and other forums across the convention. Especially in Texas and Missouri where my critics were already hysterical, he appeared to be freely using language that added fuel to the fire. It was not the fire that disturbed me, but the fuel added by my mentor and friend. At a pastors' gathering at the Van Buren Baptist Church in St. Louis, it was reported that he had announced that I had gone too far. Apparently, he suggested my book was destructive, and that it therefore was necessary to take action to preserve the Scriptures. In the supercharged atmosphere, to suggest in response to a discussion of my book and teaching that it is "necessary to preserve the Scriptures" is to imply that my book and teaching sought to destroy the Scripture. That kind of thing occurred as early as September 1961.

Even Dr. Earl Harding, the executive secretary of Missouri Baptists, a Midwestern trustee, and ultimately a strong antagonist, came to me in the early days (October-November, 1961) and indicated he found it difficult to understand some things my old teacher was saying publicly at meetings in the light of things he had said and had written to me on other occasions.[49]

Before the whole matter was finally concluded, Francisco was writing letters to my critics in Texas, indicating that I had opened a "Pandora's box." Such material was ultimately taken to the June 1962 meeting of the Southern Baptist Convention in San Francisco, and greatly contributed to the atmosphere that helped build the case against me.[50] Even that material was explained by Dr. Francisco as not being what he intended, and the confused atmosphere continued.[51] In spite of the many statements used against me because of Francisco's great popularity with various segments, there remained an underlying depth to the relationship. When I was finally dis-

---

[49]My letter to Francisco on 27 November 1961 provides a case in point.
[50]See Francisco, letter to the author, July 1962.
[51]Ibid.

missed from the faculty of Midwestern, Dr. Francisco wrote:

> Although I never agreed with your collision course, nor now with your
> decision not to delay publication of the book, I want you to know that
> I honor you for your willingness to suffer for your principles. My best
> goes out to you in this heartbreaking experience.[52]

There were many "I-told-you-so" meetings after that. It was the
depth of the relationship that made the pain so severe.

• • •

This part of the discussion began with a reflection in order to
suggest something of the hurt I was feeling in the fall of 1961 and
during the first few months of 1962. When the Midwestern Seminary
trustees appointed the seven-person investigating committee,
September 30, 1961, I met with President Berquist and L. D. Johnson,
chairman of the committee, and suggested that perhaps I should
resign because I did not want to cause the seminary problems.
However, both of them indicated that I was helping build the kind
of seminary they wanted and that to resign would do great damage.
This alleviated the pain somewhat and by the time of the meeting of
the Southern Baptist Convention in San Francisco, June 1962, I felt
strong and confident, although it was already obvious to me that
severance was likely to come within the next several months. When
the final dismissal from the seminary came, the dismissal itself was
anticlimactic.

One can lose a position or a job and there may be little agony. To
lose a friendship is another matter. The relationship with Dr.
Francisco was the deepest of those, but there were others. From the
beginning days at Midwestern Seminary, Earl Harding of the
Missouri Baptist Convention had been one of my strongest supporters. He was responsible for my invitation to numerous speaking
engagements and even stated on one occasion that my position on
Genesis agreed with his and that he had learned the approach from

---

[52]Francisco, letter to the author, 8 November 1962. This letter was written after
it was indicated that I would allow another publisher to reprint the now sold-out
book.

Dr. H. E. Dana at Central Baptist Theological Seminary, and that it was nothing new to him.[53] Harding's support held until the political pressures began to build, but then the doublespeak disease became standard operating procedure. Evidently some people want to be on everyone's side. Discovering such duplicity in what is thought to be a genuine relationship of integrity causes much agony. Reflection upon this procedure helps me understand how some of the so-called "moderate" leaders in the current Southern Baptist struggle have at times been on both sides, and that as early as 1962.

I should hasten to add, however, that in all probability the reason the temporary pain of that early period did not turn into depression was because I was energized by the tremendous unsolicited support from lay people, from students, and from some pastors. Added to this was the wonderful support of the Calvary Baptist Church in Kansas City where I was a member. That story must be delayed until a later time, but it is most important to applaud the support that turned a "down" moment into a time of a great sense of mission and purpose. The "church" can disappoint us at times, but it was the community of faith called Calvary Baptist Church that gave me nurture and strength.

As I have hinted before, what amazed me was that the lay people some of the preachers were seeking to protect were so very supportive and appreciative. Their letters helped me to believe I was contributing to their liberation and that I was helping to broaden their faith and their appreciation for the Bible. My stability and firm conviction about what I was doing was particularly boosted by a letter from a Mrs. W. W. Wheeler of Deer Park, Texas, a letter that came at the "right" moment in my life. It was the Kairos catalyst for a strength which saw me through. In part, Mrs. Wheeler wrote:

> I do not have a theological education and so perhaps do not have a right to an opinion on a theological book. But I like *The Message of Genesis* very much. If I had read it twenty-five years ago, it might have spared me many years of doubting. It took me a long time to learn that religious truth can be conveyed in a variety of literary media. And so

---

[53]See my letter to Harding, 16 February 1962.

long as our preachers yelp every time somebody says that the Bible does not have to be interpreted literally, so will our young people have to struggle with a conflict that does not really exist—and many of them will be lost forever as far as our denomination is concerned. You have done us a real service, and I hope you will not let the furor keep you from writing more.[54]

Such letters concretized my purpose and infused stamina. I thought the receipt of such letters—many of them—was most remarkable. What is even more remarkable to me is that although I have been removed from Southern Baptist life for many years, such letters are even yet periodically received. During the time I was writing the present manuscript, I have been in correspondence through a series of letters with a lady in Tennessee, and the tenor of the comments are the same. Occasionally even now, when I will not have thought of *The Message of Genesis* or the controversy for months and months, the telephone will ring and a person known or unknown to me will share a similar message to that of those early letters. Surely we have done the people in our churches a huge disservice in failing to recognize their hunger and their capacity to grapple with the deepest issues of life and meaning. Those early letters encouraged me to believe, and experience has confirmed the belief that the people in our churches do contemplate life's deepest questions, struggle with theology as the reflective dimension of piety, and reach conclusions characterized by insight and maturity. Often they keep their musings to themselves for fear their expressions may not sound as orthodox as their clergy overseers would desire. The correspondence of those days, again comparing lay and clergy writers, caused me to believe that some clergy use orthodox jargon as a cover-up for having failed to do the hard thinking characteristic of some of the lay people. Lay people are willing to share life's questions; clergy often think they have some kind of mandate to share only answers. Some have learned the basic wisdom:

Be patient toward all that is unsolved in your heart . . . try to love the

---

[54]Wheeler, letter to the author, 6 February 1962.

questions themselves like locked rooms and like books that are written in a very foreign tongue. Do not now seek the answers, which cannot be given you because you would not be able to live with them. And the point is, to live everything. Live the questions now. Perhaps you will then gradually, without noticing it, live along some distant day into the answer.[55]

The assistance of students also gave my courage sinew, clarity, and direction. At the risk of appearing to be self-serving, I share a letter from a student that came during that July-December 1961 period. There were many such letters, but the one I share is indicative of so many nuances that were very important to me at the time. This particular letter was addressed to Dr. Conrad Willard, chairman, board of trustees, with copies to Dr. Berquist and to me:

I have been rather surprised and disappointed at the large amount of publicity that I have been hearing and reading concerning the teachings of Dr. Ralph Elliott.

First, I would like to say that I am and will always be grateful that God allowed my wife and me the privilege of sitting under Dr. Elliott's teaching and that of the other professors at Midwestern Seminary. I came from the livestock business to the seminary in 1958. I was a lamb that could easily have been devoured by "the heretical type of person" that publicity is assigning to Dr. Ralph Elliott. This, however, was not the case. During my first semester at Midwestern, I had Hebrew and Old Testament Survey from Dr. Elliott and Biblical Archaeology from Dr. Morton and New Testament from Dr. McClain. This was a trying time in my life because I was fighting a call to the foreign mission field. It was through the teachings of Dr. Elliott and Dr. Morton and private conferences with them that I was able to find God's leadership in a deeper way than I had previously known. Thus, on the first Missionary Day I went forward to surrender to world mission.

During my second year at the seminary I took advanced Hebrew under Dr. Elliott. I had learned to appreciate his method of teaching although he required hard work from his students. However, he does not require anything of his students that he is not willing to give

---

[55]Rainer Maria Rilke, "Living the Questions," frontispiece in Robert A. Raines, *Living the Questions* (Waco TX: Word Books, 1976).

himself and his first interest is to help each student help himself in the search for truth. He requires his students to look to the right and to the left, to read widely and then to find a path that they themselves can walk.

This past year I was privileged to sit in Dr. Elliott's class in Old Testament Theology. I have seldom been in a revival meeting where God's presence was as strong. His teachings on the theological message of Genesis helped me to gain rather than lose my Bible. This insight has enabled me to gain personal strength from God's presence and to preach with more power than before. This was without a doubt the most outstanding course that I took at Midwestern Seminary. I wish that every minister in the Southern Baptist convention could have studied through this course.

In my mind there is no doubt that Dr. Ralph Elliott was sent by God to head the Old Testament Department of Midwestern Seminary and that I was sent by the same God to sit at the feet of Dr. Elliott to be prepared for the difficult task of trying to be God's servant to the Moslem people of East Pakistan.

I feel that I am voicing not only my convictions but also the convictions of my fellow students who have taken advanced courses under Dr. Elliott which has enabled us to more fully evaluate him as a Christian and as a teacher. I have held back voicing my feeling because I felt that the things I was reading and hearing were only strands of the truth twisted to leave a false impression and I saw no necessity of defending truth. However, there has been so much said by those who have not had the privilege of the many class hours under Dr. Elliott that I felt it my duty to pass along my personal testimony of what I have seen and heard.[56]

With such encouragement and the assurance that my own life was of significance through what I was sharing and in relationship with my students, one can understand that the pain referred to earlier was in a context of broad meaning and that the ensuing months were as steps on an important pilgrimage.

The focus of the above has been on persons from the churches and certain students. This combination provided sustenance

---

[56]Carl F. Ryther, graduating class of 1961, letter to Conrad Willard, Midwestern's board of trustees chairman, 20 December 1961.

throughout the pilgrimage, as will be more clearly noted when the contributions of a group called Baptists for Freedom are noted. This supportive organization came into being under the leadership of students Robert Latham, Edward Damer, John C. Bush, and Joseph R. Frazier, and laymen Harry Reyburn and Robert Woodruff. The encouragement of this particular group will receive attention later as will the support of the Calvary Baptist Church in Kansas City. I can only marvel at the providence of God in making support available at the various twists in life's journey.

## 5. The Prelude to San Francisco

Hopefully, the interlude has provided perspective and context. We must be reminded now, however, that actions bring reactions and further actions, one influencing another.

The first noticeable effect from the pressure created by the March 1962 Oklahoma City caucus meeting was the equivocation of the Sunday School Board of the Southern Baptist Convention. Although unknown to me at the time and without notice to me, in less than one month following the Oklahoma meeting, and without public announcement, an internal decision was made that *The Message of Genesis* would not be reprinted nor would there be another edition. It seems that James L. Sullivan, executive secretary-treasurer of the board, became frightened by the furor surrounding the book, in spite of the bold stand taken by the board in January of the same year, defending the board's right to publish the book. Therefore, Sullivan exercised what he said was executive privilege and gave oral instruction that no reprint be authorized without his personal approval.[57] For all practical purposes, the book was banned by executive fiat.

Although this decision was made on April 5, 1962, I can only assume that knowledge of it was held as privileged information by a very small inner circle. Apparently, it was not communicated even to the book editor of Broadman Press because he continued to

---

[57]See Reuben E. Alley, "Evasion and Appeasement," *The Religious Herald* 135 (8 November 1962) and a personal letter from Gomer Lesch, an executive assistant to Sullivan, to Sally Rice, 1 March 1963.

negotiate with me for a reprinting of the book. The contract with the publisher indicated the book would be reprinted as long as it was in demand, and, thanks to the controversy, it was certainly in demand. (Facetiously I have suggested that I have written other books, but the publisher's stock was seldom exhausted because no one was willing to start a campaign against them. Criticism does sell books.)

On April 18, 1962, almost two weeks following Sullivan's decision, William Fallis of Broadman Press wrote to me concerning the reprinting:

> As of last Friday, sales had reached 3,184 copies, with 200 being sold during the first two weeks of this month. If this rate continues, we will need to reprint the book within the next six to eight weeks, and we will be needing your correction copy in the near future. Can you return it by May 7?[58]

Fallis also offered me the option of revising any statements in the book if I wished to do so.

On April 24, 1962, I wrote to Dr. Fallis and indicated that I would return the materials and any changes to his office prior to May 7. At the same time, I indicated there would be no major changes:

> [I]n view of the situation at the moment, I do not believe it would be wise to make any editorial changes or to revise any statements. Though I cannot elaborate upon them, I have been offered many "deals" by various critical groups if I would make revisions. Thus, I am afraid that any revisions which I would make at the present time would indicate capitulation. This would have a sense of victory to a group which I feel does not need to be encouraged at this particular moment.[59]

In all of my relationships with Dr. Fallis, I found him to be most honorable. I do not believe he knew of the intrigue within the inner circle. It is but one more of many indications of the scheming and maneuvering. Immediately after the book was published, a daily tally of letters for and letters against the book was kept in Nashville. The major concern was that nothing disturb the Cooperative

---

[58]Fallis, letter to the author, 18 April 1962.
[59]Elliott to Fallis, 24 April 1962.

Program receipts. I was well aware of that concern and can understand something of Dr. Sullivan's fear, although the way he handled it, especially the secrecy and duplicity allowed in continuing negotiations with me for a reprint, was less than honorable. Of course, I do not know what kind of threats and political pressures Dr. Sullivan was experiencing in his office. I suspect there were many. I cannot verify the truth of the matter, but it has been reported to me that Dr. Sullivan indicated to some that he wrote the "true" story of all of these matters, a story to be shared at some point only after his death. Many pressures are placed upon the Sunday School Board in an effort to assure its orthodoxy, as recently again became evident in the 1991 resignation of Lloyd Elder as the executive of that board.

In light of the many efforts of the antagonists, I wrote to a friend on March 31, 1962 that I thought the June 1962 annual meeting of the Southern Baptist Convention at San Francisco might write the final chapter. My reasoning was as follows:

> When one considers that Texas contributes about one-quarter of all the funds which are channeled, for instance, through the Foreign Mission Board, one can understand something of the seriousness of the situation. Whether we like it or not, money has a great deal to do with the general reaction.[60]

As we moved towards the June 5-8 convention in San Francisco, charges and countercharges continued in furious fashion, in editorials, in letters, and by telephone. The January-June 1962 propaganda campaign had its impact. Many assumed San Francisco would be a "showdown," and such was promoted by those who had been at the March Oklahoma City caucus. In addition to the impact upon Dr. Sullivan to alter the regular process of the Sunday School Board, other rumors from that quarter suggested fear was abroad. This, too, related specifically to the Sunday School Board executive. I mention it here because I believe that in the final analysis three key figures had much to do with the final "solution." Clyde T. Francisco's ambivalence and his willing or unwilling provision of

---

[60]Elliott, letter to T. Herbert Gilmore, 31 March 1962.

material that was so widely used by the critics has been discussed. The weight of Herschel Hobbs's office as president of the convention and how he used that power with reference to Midwestern is forthcoming. The other party is James L. Sullivan. That these three should have such important negative roles regarding the upholding of freedom is a paradox: they were *not* in theological agreement with the leaders of the controversy.

I am certain Dr. Sullivan must have had terrible pressure placed upon him. Some of the chief antagonists in the entire fracas—Mack Douglas for one—were on the Sunday School Board. It is only human to need a way out, and Sullivan's attempt to remove himself from the eye of the storm began to be apparent to me.

Broadman Press had accepted the book on its own merits with pressure from no one. The word that began to be circulated from the executive secretary's office, however, was that the book was published only because Midwestern Seminary had asked for it as a textbook, and that it otherwise would not have been published. It was further suggested that Midwestern's request would withdraw the book from further sale or publication since it was published at the institution's insistence. This was as disturbing to me as anything that had happened because it was absolutely false, and in my mind represented one more effort to escape any responsibility or implied blame during a difficult time. The process of publication was not at all as suggested by the executive secretary's office. The pinpointing of Midwestern Seminary overlooks the fact that the book was initiated while the author was a faculty member at Southern Seminary and in response to a Broadman Press representative's request that some faculty member write something in the field of critical-theological understanding. The hope was that the book would appeal to students, pastors, and thinking lay people. My recollection is that the *only* indication it would be used as a textbook was by Southern Seminary.

One can only conclude that the Sunday School Board, through its chief executive, was seeking to redirect the fire and to contain any damage that might already have been done. Whatever the motivation, this waffling weakened the positive environment and certainly contributed to the ultimate actions at the convention. Dr. Sullivan's role during the convention itself is still a matter of controversy.

## 6. The 1962 Southern Baptist Convention Annual Meeting

I suppose the meeting of the Southern Baptist Convention in San Francisco, June 5-8, 1962, had as much ultimate impact on the remainder of my life—how and where it was to be spent—as any other one thing. Nevertheless, I was a rather innocent spectator at the convention. Much of it was about me, but there was little opportunity for me to touch what was happening. It was the first time I had had any exposure to big-time politics. The closest I had come to it was in student government politics in high school days, and there was no comparison.

Convention attendance itself was something new to me. The small churches I served in Tennessee, Illinois, and Kentucky during student days did not have the financial means to send a pastor to the annual meeting. As a seminary professor, my own funds were limited and the encouragement of professor attendance at the convention meetings was not a priority of the seminaries. This was my *first* convention. It is perhaps ironic that my attendance at this convention was not as a representative of the seminary but as a messenger from Calvary Baptist Church of Kansas City which I was serving as interim pastor. It was an eye-opening experience.

From the preconvention Pastors' Conference to the very end, I learned of such political maneuvering as how to remove trustees and fix the future, and such political facts that orthodoxy is stronger than love and that friends look for cover when the storms come. (Perhaps my best San Francisco experience was being introduced to English muffins for breakfast, then a novelty for me, a happenstance that has provided routine breakfast context from then until now.)

Although I watched the convention antics as a spectator and neither sought to speak in my own behalf nor was asked to do so, I did not feel intimidated nor did I experience anxiety about the future. I was concerned that the affairs of the Kingdom could be sullied by people pursuing selfish interests in a power game, but somehow knew that God is God and that God knows the way through the wilderness.

I do remember telephoning my wife to explain to her the ping-pong-ball experience of being the subject, directly or indirectly, of multiple motions which were carried over from one session to the next. It was like watching myself being thrown from one court to another, helpless to intervene. I had not known before that it was possible to be both subject and observer, attached to yourself and yet displaced from yourself. It was a weird experience to "watch" my life being played out in the public arena. One thing was obvious as events developed from session to session, namely, that the threads woven by the Oklahoma caucus were now being gathered into a tapestry that made it fairly easy to guess the prognosis for the future. What I thought to be an immediate future, however, had overtones for a distant future in whose scenario the Southern Baptist Convention finds itself today.

Existentially, the more important of the two main threads might have been the discussion and the actions surrounding the banning or not banning of *The Message of Genesis*. Actually, the more important thread for the distant future was the surfacing of preconvention planning to take over a seminary and ultimately the convention itself. It is this latter that continues to be lived out in current history. That a person was made expendable in the process had its pain. That others were wittingly and unwittingly used as tools has hindsight confirmation, although the apparent nature of such seemed present at the moment.

The two threads to which I have made reference are the book episode and the trustee episode. It is necessary to give focus to the book first, but the impact for posterity requires the recognition that the focus on the book in fact involved the preconceived and long-range plans to take over an institution and a convention. Motives are generally multiple, and those held by people who thought they were saving God's Kingdom and those who deliberately were seeking to build their own kingdom drew a mixed assortment of people into concerted action. Personalities and institutions, functionaries and agencies were sucked into the vortex of the whirlwind. Those involvements were actualized in the twofold display of the convention and the book, and the convention and the trustees.

*a. The Convention and the Book.* The hindsight of history appears to have demonstrated that the main goal of the group critical of Midwestern Seminary was to replace certain trustees with "safe" ones. There is the evidence of record that indicates there was a major campaign toward that end. The book in dispute was but one piece of their distaste for the leadership, faculty, and perspective of the seminary. The book, however, was the flying wedge for opening the fray.

Plans had been made at the caucus meeting in Oklahoma City to bring the matter of the affairs at Midwestern to the convention floor. This was confirmed when some 100 men met in a downtown San Francisco motel on the evening of June 5, 1962. Ross Edwards—the former Central Seminary trustee who was disappointed that his anticipated administrative role at Midwestern had not materialized—presided. A motion was framed for the convention, and K. Owen White was selected as spokesperson to present the motion. There was some discussion as to whether the motion should deal with the book in a frontal attack or whether the better move would be an oblique attack around the issue of biblical authority. They chose the latter, perhaps for a practical reason—Who would want to be accused of banning books in a free society?—and because they believed, one assumes, that the book denied biblical authority as they understood it.

The precaucus gathering was called a stormy session,[61] and no doubt it was, because the right wing had been ignited by the address of J. Sidlow Baxter at the Pastors' Conference. His speech was not a head-on attack, but rather a carefully crafted innuendo slingshot with jargon tailor-made for the occasion. There was little doubt as to where the arrow was intended when he plucked his bow to the delight of the crowd:

> We Baptists have been champions of the duty of private judgment, but liberty to interpret the Bible never meant to discredit the Bible.[62]

The implication of course was that the Bible was being discredited,

---

[61]Gainer Bryan, "Southern Baptists Hold Stormy Session," *The Maryland Baptist* 45 (14 June 1962) 5.

[62]Jim Newton, "Pastors Evidence Concern for Theological Position," *Baptist Standard* 84 (13 June 1962) 14.

and the agenda was to remove the discreditor and to punish the institution giving sanctuary to the one(s) doing the discrediting.

According to plan, on the first full day of the convention K. Owen White presented the following motion, which was approved by an overwhelming standing vote:

> I move that the messengers to this convention, by standing vote, reaffirm their faith in the *entire* Bible as the authoritative, authentic, infallible word of God, that we express our abiding and unchanging objection to the dissemination of the theological views in any of our seminaries which would undermine such faith in the historical accuracy and doctrinal integrity of the Bible, and that we kindly but firmly instruct the trustees and administrative officers of our institutions and (other) agencies to take such steps as shall be necessary to remedy at once those situations where such views now threaten our historic position.[63]

Someone from the floor called to the attention of Convention President Herschel Hobbs that bylaw 12 of the Convention rules required that unscheduled motions not receiving unanimous support be referred to the Committee on Order of Business for scheduling at a future time.

K. Owen White was soon followed by Ralph F. Powell, a pastor from Kansas City, who represented a small group from the previous night's caucus who desired to follow a different strategy, taking a frontal rather than an oblique attack. This was the same Ralph Powell who had said over a Kansas City radio station that three crosses should be erected—"one for Bishop Oxnam, one for Bishop Pike, and one for Ralph Elliott."[64] At least I was in good company.

(Powell's radio address was credited by police as possibly the thing that stirred some would-be protectors of God and Bible to throw an explosive device from a speeding automobile, partially demolishing the front door of my house in Kansas City. That

---

[63]*Southern Baptist Convention Bulletin* 39 (7 June 1962) 3, third day.

[64]Bishops Oxnam and Pike were bishops in the Methodist and Episcopal Churches, respectively, and were known for open minds and liberal positions on some matters.

comment over the airways may also have had something to do with the decision of radio stations KBEA and KBEV to name me "man of the week" with an appropriate certificate *in November, 1962.)*

Powell presented the following motion which was likewise referred to the Committee on Order of Business under bylaw 12:

> I recommend that this convention instruct the Sunday School Board to cease from publication and printing the book *The Message of Genesis*, by Dr. Elliott, and that they furthermore recall from all sales this book which contradicts Baptist conviction.[65]

The announcement subsequently was made that these two motions would be included in the order of business on Thursday morning. This resulted in a huge attendance at the Thursday morning session. There obviously had been some politicking during the night, for President Hobbs ruled that White's motion was in reality two motions and would be considered as such. The first motion was, therefore, a motion to affirm faith in the Bible. It was quite interesting to observe the host of messengers who were watching to see how I would vote. I think I shocked some and disappointed others in voting *for* White's motion. It was something of a dilemma for me because it was obvious that the original purpose of the motion was for my condemnation. However, I did and do respond with enthusiasm to the authentic and authoritative Bible, and desired to be counted on record. I believe the vote of the huge crowd present was unanimous. Today I would have more of a problem with the way the motion was stated and there are some theological niceties that bother me, for I view Christ, and not the Bible, as ultimate authority.

The remainder of White's original motion now constituted a second motion, and it engendered lengthy debate and many requests for the interpretation of certain words and phrases used in the motion. This debate became ugly at times, and a great Baptist statesman was abused and mistreated by the ever-so-orthodox but ever-so-unloving crowd. I think most of those present did not know or did not remember the phrases from Ephesians 1:15: "faith in the

---

[65]*Southern Baptist Convention Bulletin* 39 (7 June 1962) 3, third day.

Lord Jesus and . . . love toward all the saints."

Dr. Wallace Bassett, a gracious gentleman of the old school and longtime pastor of the Cliff Temple Baptist Church in Dallas, Texas, and claiming to be the oldest person to speak at the convention, sought to put the motion in what he believed to be a historical perspective. Whether he was right or wrong in his perspective, it was tragic to see a faithful servant so rudely treated by being booed and loudly shouted down. According to Dr. Bassett, the motion as presented represented a "creed-making effort" similar to that of the J. Frank Norris days when a splinter group of fundamentalists attacked the convention, withdrew, and continued the attack in a newly constituted denomination.[66] The motion was finally passed with a large majority vote in the following form:

> That we express our abiding and unchanging objection to the dissemi-
> nation of theological views in any of our seminaries which would
> undermine such faith in the historical accuracy and doctrinal integrity
> of the Bible, and that we courteously request the trustees and adminis-
> trative officers of our institutions and other agencies to take such steps
> as shall be necessary to remedy at once those situations where such
> views now threaten our historic position.[67]

Upon returning home from the convention, Dr. Bassett wrote me a letter in which he elaborated upon his convention statement before the noise made it impossible to continue, and suggested, "I don't agree with many things in the book." His comments in the letter were:

> A few of your conclusions I do not accept—not because they are too
> liberal, but too conservative. I go much further than you do in some
> things.[68]

It is of more than passing interest to me that people who received their training in Southern Baptist institutions at an earlier period,

---

[66]I find it of interest that the group now in control of the Southern Baptist Convention has received back into its fold and restored to fellowship the denominational inheritors of the J. Frank Norris "heresy."

[67]As reported in *The Religious Herald*, 14 June 1962, 13.

[68]Bassett, letter to the author, 26 June 1962.

represented by Dr. Bassett and some even earlier, had a much more understanding approach to the nature of the biblical revelation and were broader in their views. I corresponded with a number of these older men, men like Dr. W. R. Cullum, age ninety-five in 1962 and for forty-two years head of the School of the Bible at Wake Forest College; Dr. S. L. Morgan, age ninety-plus in 1962; and Dr. William Harrison Williams, a student at Southern Baptist Theological Seminary 1901-1904 and son of the famous Southern Seminary professor of that name. Dr. Williams indicated that he sat under the teaching of the great men of the 1900s era of the seminary and that he had always held the general positions that now were being criticized. In addition to letters, Dr. Williams and Dr. Morgan affirmed their more open views in a February 22, 1962 issue of the *Religious Herald*, the Virginia Baptist newspaper. The following statement by William Harrison Williams, honored North Carolina pastor, shows something of the contrast between that of the 1960s and a much earlier period:

> I have my father's scrapbook in which he has preserved a statement made to the seminary by Dr. C. H. Toy in 1879. As I read his statement, I marvel at the fact that there is not a Bible teacher in our schools or seminaries who would not heartily subscribe to his position which was, "language is language and we should seek to find what the Bible really says," and yet we vanquished from the ranks the most brilliant scholars Southern Baptists ever had.[69]

This was not, however, the comprehension of historic tradition understood by the 105th session of the Southern Baptist Convention meeting in San Francisco, and the mood was definitely of a different sort. What happened might be better characterized by the second half of a comment from Jaroslav Pelikan, that "tradition is the living faith of the dead; traditionalism is the dead faith of the living."[70] With reference to *The Message of Genesis*, the most interesting part of the convention followed the action on the White motions. The

---

[69]Williams, letter to the author, 2 February 1962.
[70]Pelikan, *The Vindication of Tradition* (New Haven CT: Yale University Press, 1984) 65.

resolution presented by Ralph Powell was significant in and of itself, but even more significant in terms of some of the political bargaining it revealed. Actually, there were two motions to ban the book, Powell's and one offered by Ben D. Windham of Oregon. The one by Powell had the more significant ramifications.

Powell's motion, first introduced on Wednesday, was referred by the Committee on Order of Business to the Thursday morning session. When time came for consideration of the motion, Earl Harding, executive secretary of the Missouri Baptist Convention (Powell's convention), stepped to the microphone and requested that Mr. Powell withdraw his motion. The presentation of the motion had violated the strategy developed by the continuation of the Oklahoma caucus group. It is understood that Harding had been reasoning with Powell early in the morning and sharing an explanation of the group's larger strategy and ultimate goal—not just to remove a professor and a book, but to gain influence over a seminary and an entire convention. Powell reluctantly agreed, but not before stating to the convention that:

> Not out of cowardice, in spite of my conviction to the contrary, in the spirit of cooperation, with the understanding that I have the right to present it again if I feel so led, because I respect the leadership of the man who leads us in Missouri, I withdraw my motion.[71]

There are two connections of great interest here. The first is that Earl Harding was most concerned that the caucus group not be charged with book banning. It was considered that such an image would weaken the influence of those who had plotted the strategy. The concern that the group not be tainted with such an image surfaced again in a procedural meeting with Midwestern's board of trustees one week before I was dismissed, October 18, 1963. The elaboration of the point will be clearer if we wait until the meeting is discussed in detail. It is sufficient here to say that the board of trustees extracted from me an agreement not to allow the book to be reprinted if they, as my employers, gave me an order to that effect.

---

[71]See Gainer Bryan, "Southern Baptists Hold Stormy Session," *Maryland Baptist*, 14 June 1962, 2-11.

In spite of the excitement of some of the trustees that this might solve the problems, and in spite of my agreement to abide by such a decision, Harding asked for and carried the day, on a reconsideration because he did not wish to be accused of being a book-banner and he also felt that such would reflect poorly on the trustees.

The other consideration involves Dr. Herschel Hobbs, president of the convention, and Dr. James L. Sullivan, executive secretary-treasurer of the Sunday School Board. Dr. Sullivan, of course, had already given an administrative order that any further plans for the reprinting of the book be suspended until further notice. At this point in the chronology, Dr. Hobbs may have honestly viewed himself as the reconciler of the many factions. Later, as I shall indicate elsewhere, my conclusion was that he definitely committed himself to a particular point of view. That point had not yet arrived, and so in an effort to help me understand what had gone on in the process about the book banning, he informed me in personal conversation that Dr. Harding and Mr. Powell had conferred with him about Powell's motion. Dr. Sullivan was also brought into the conversation. According to Hobbs, Sullivan promised there would be no more books if the motion were withdrawn. Some of the public display was thus time-consuming playacting because backroom private commitments had been made. Backroom politics is not something relegated to congressional chambers in Washington.

Of course, not many were privy to such information, so on Thursday afternoon another effort was made. Mr. Windham of Oregon moved:

> That this convention instruct the Sunday School Board to cease publishing and to recall from all distribution channels the book, *The Message of Genesis*, by Ralph Elliott.[72]

The Committee on Order of Business scheduled consideration of the motion on Thursday evening. There was a very strong debate, and the strange turn of events that led to the defeat of the motion was the vehement opposition by Dr. E. S. James, editor of the *Baptist Standard* of Texas and one of my severest and most frequent critics.

---

[72]"Proceedings," *Annual of the Southern Baptist Convention 1962*, article 91, 69.

James's argument against the motion was not because he had a change of heart, but because he felt it would be a bad precedent to instruct an agency of the denomination as to its direction. He asked that we "leave our agencies free to make the decision, and let's criticize them if they make the wrong one."[73] The approach James took was most inconsistent with his willingness to instruct seminaries which are denominational agencies under Southern Baptist control. James, Harding, and many others in that camp were very much concerned that they not be accused of violating the Baptist tradition of freedom. The public and private stance was often quite contrary. Many times I was told they believed in freedom, and that meant that if I could not agree with their viewpoints, "I was free to leave and seek employment elsewhere."

Mr. Windham did not give up easily, and it took some thirty additional minutes of floor debate, but the capstone for the motion's defeat was added when G. Allen West, pastor of Nashville's Woodmont Baptist Church, said that "we do not believe in book burning and yet we are about to practice something here which goes back to the fifteenth century."[74]

Some who helped defeat the motion were "friends," but the strongest call for its defeat came from those who were in sympathy with the caucus movement. In addition to its violation of their strategy, there seemed to be great concern lest the Southern Baptist Convention give to the world the feeling it was living in an earlier century. There seemed to be little realization that the hue and cry they had raised had already made Southern Baptists appear to most of the world as obscurantists. Officially, these people were not book-banners, but the president of the convention appears to have entered into a secret deal to ban the book. Later when an effort was made to get the plates of the book so another publisher could take up the project, it appeared for a while that the decision to ban the book was fixed in stone because the plates initially were unavailable. From the vantage point of later years, I suspect that I personally would have

---

[73]Cf. "Convention Votes Not to Ban Elliott's Book," as recorded from the Baptist Press news release and reported in the *Biblical Recorder*, 16 June 1962, 6.
   [74]Ibid.

fared better had the motion to ban the book been formally passed. The quiet internal arrangements deflected public pressure from the convention functionaries.

   *b. The Convention and the Trustees.* Of more interest than the book to *all* of us at Midwestern Seminary was the question of the composition of the board of trustees. The book was but one item of concern. The makeup of the board of trustees affected academic freedom, freedom of expression, the direction of the seminary, and all the rest. Since the March 1961 Oklahoma City caucus meeting, there had been diligent effort to remove from the board, even when eligible for reelection, those who had sustained me at the special December 1961 board meeting. The venom was directed towards a true saint, seminary President Millard Berquist. Berquist had made it quite clear up to this point that he championed the direction the seminary had taken. Rumors had circulated since March 1962 that members of the Oklahoma caucus were putting extreme pressure on the Committee on Committees of the Southern Baptist Convention to replace outgoing trustees who had been favorable to me with others who would be against me. Twelve vacancies were to be filled. Six of the spots could have been filled with men who were eligible for reelection. However, four of the six eligibles were replaced.

   To get ahead of the story, it is worth noting that of the twelve people elected at the San Francisco Convention, nine voted for my dismissal, and a tenth one voted for dismissal when an appeal for unity was made. I can readily understand why faculty members of the various Southern Baptist seminaries have watched with such eagerness the trustee election process in recent years.

   Sally Rice, at the time a student in the Duke University Department of Religion, made a study of the apparent pressure tactics used, and sought to engage in correspondence with the four trustees who were eligible for reelection but were not reelected. The four were Edward L. Byrd, South Carolina; Truman Aldredge, Louisiana; Woodson Armes, Texas; and Clayton Deering, Oklahoma. Each was asked whether he felt his position on the "Elliott issue" had anything to do with his failure to be renominated by the Committee on Committees. Clayton Deering of Oklahoma was the only one who failed to respond.[75]

However, prior to the San Francisco Convention, Dr. Clayton Deering telephoned us at the seminary (via President Berquist) to say he had had a "showdown" with the Oklahoma man on the Committee on Committees and had been told that he would be renominated if he would agree to change his vote on the Elliott business. Deering told me he therefore would not be going back on the board for he could not change his vote. Deering found himself in a very untenable position for which survival necessitated the maintenance of the goodwill of the Oklahoma churches and pastors. I fully understood his predicament, and hardly see how he could have done other than he did. I appreciate the pain and the anxiety which the situation placed upon him.

Woodson Armes of Texas indicated that all he knew about the politics of the Oklahoma group was what he read in the papers. He indicated he had not attended the December 1961 board meeting at Midwestern, that he was not bothered by the failure to be renominated, and that he knew little of what was transpiring.[76] The noncommittal nature of Armes's answers created the feeling that he had been tampered with.

Byrd and Aldredge were quite forthright. Both had interesting stories. Byrd's position on the Genesis issue was a matter of written record. Knowing he would be unable to attend the December 1961 trustee meeting when the Elliott matter was to be considered, he wrote President Berquist about his views. He indicated his support for the approach to the Scriptures used in *The Message of Genesis*, stated his agreement with most of the conclusions in the book, and championed the right of freedom of expression. Following a letter to him by the Oklahoma caucus group, Byrd was visited by the South Carolina representative of the Committee on Committees. The specific purpose of the visit was to inquire about his position on the Elliott matter. Although the representative made it clear they wanted

---

[75]Sally Rice, "Ralph Elliott: Controversial Figure among Southern Baptists," a paper submitted to the Duke University Department of Religion (15 April 1963) 43-45.
    [76]Ibid., 45.

to nominate trustees who were against Elliott, Byrd felt that he had made a case for his position and that the South Carolina delegate was favorably disposed towards him. Nevertheless, when the committee was convened for the San Francisco meeting, the South Carolina representative nominated someone else. Byrd was most candid in giving his appraisal of the situation:

> I would say that my attitude toward Dr. Elliott was the one and only reason I was not renominated to the board. Incidentally, I was the vice president of the board, and presumably would have been made president since the president had moved from Kansas City to Miami and was no longer the Missouri member of the board.[77]

Dr. Aldredge had a similar experience. Apparently, trustees who opposed Aldredge's pro-Elliott stance at the December 1961 board meeting immediately circulated the word that "certain people needed to be convinced." Dr. Aldredge received many letters after the December meeting, letters which reprimanded him because of his vote and threatened him with the loss of his trusteeship. The Louisiana member of the Committee on Committees was bombarded with anti-Elliott material. This representative fiercely fought Aldredge's possible renomination and demonstrated an extremely negative attitude. What the chairman of the Committee on Committees called the "ugliest attitude of anyone on the committee" may have been in part due to his association with one of the earliest critics, Mack Douglas of St. Louis. Douglas held a revival in the committee member's Louisiana church just prior to the San Francisco convention. In response to Sally Rice's question, Aldredge wrote, in part:

> To answer your question, I feel positively that my attitude toward Dr. Elliott was THE reason why I was not renominated. I was told by the chairman of the Committee on Boards that there were members of this committee who sought the renomination of these five (correction: four) trustees and who pinned the opposition down to this one specific reason, making them admit that this, and this alone, was the reason for

---

[77]Ibid.

failure to vote for renomination.[78]

Today the use of the Committee on Committees to gain control of an institution or institutions has been loudly claimed by such people as Paul Pressler and those who have worked with him in plotting the takeover of the Southern Baptist Convention. It was a new phenomenon in 1962, and some saw the prospects for the future as being less than pleasant. Editor C. R. Daley of the *Western Recorder*, Kentucky Baptist paper, felt the discovery that such reported conniving was real would be deplorable.[79]

Daley's editorial, "A Decision of Destiny," was surely more prophetic than he himself knew. One can only wonder, however, why the tactics caught everyone with such surprise. Shortly after the announced intentions of those who attended the March 1962 Oklahoma City caucus meeting and two and one-half months prior to San Francisco, the brave editor of the Baptist paper in Louisiana had objected to the "applied pressure on the nominating committee in an effort to attack the board of trustees of Midwestern" and described such tactics as "dirty pool" and "stacking the deck."[80] Prior to the San Francisco meeting, Editor John J. Hurt of Georgia had said that "Southern Baptists will learn the difference between the two words 'cooperate' and 'dictate' within the next two months, or they will disgrace themselves in annual convention come June 4."[81]

## 7. Convention Reflections

Apparently, however, only a few sensed the ominous future that would develop from the seedlings sprouted in San Francisco. I was personally concerned about the larger future because I saw how easy it was to utilize crowd control under skillful instrumentation. Members of the press who sought me out in San Francisco indicated that when they stationed survey people at the various exits of the convention center after a negative vote, although they spoke with

---

[78]Ibid.
[79]Daley, "A Decision of Destiny," *Western Recorder*, 27 September 1962, 4.
[80]James F. Cole, *Baptist Message*, 15 March 1962.
[81]Hurt, *Christian Index*, 29 March 1962.

hundreds and hundreds of people who had voted with the right wing, they could only find twenty-five people who had read any part of *The Message of Genesis*. They were persuaded by the hysteria abroad. Some parts of the establishment, like the Baptist Sunday School Board, began to run for cover in order to protect its flanks. Many others engaged in a kind of self-congratulation that peace had been bought and that the convention did not split. The two attitudes, congratulatory relief and self-preservation, are best seen in the evolution of President Herschel Hobbs's role at the convention and the Sunday School Board's actions following the convention.

    *a. Congratulatory Relief.* As I sat next to a colleague listening to Herschel Hobbs's presidential address, I scribbled a note to my friend indicating that Hobbs's speech seemed to be a kind of camouflage and that it would "help to sell us out." Since Hobbs had on a recent visit with us at Midwestern indicated that he was such a strong friend to the faculty, I also noted my sadness that a "friend" was helping to lay the groundwork for my own demise. It is possible, of course, that my perspective was so motivated by a defensive point of view that I was misreading and mishearing. Unfortunately, postconvention events appeared to me to confirm my judgment because I believe to this very day that it was pressure exerted by Dr. Hobbs on Dr. Berquist that ultimately changed him from a very bold and courageous "here-I-stand" position to capitulation in order to "save the seminary." This followed a command visit by Berquist and me to Hobbs's office in Oklahoma City. That visit and its aftermath will be reported in proper sequence.

    It is true, nonetheless, that at the time, many viewed Herschel Hobbs, because of his address and the manner in which he administered the San Francisco Convention, as being the savior of the denomination. In his presidential address, "Crisis and Conquest," he gave much attention to the theological crisis in which the denomination found itself and attributed the crisis to an invasion by physical science and philosophy, thus contributing to the "modern liberalism" we were experiencing. To set the Genesis debate in the context of modern liberalism and to indicate sympathy with the anti-intellectualism that was so much a part of the Southern Baptist struggle helped to fan the flames and gave encouragement to those opponents who already were on a "new high," having been pumped up by the mostly divisive twenty-five addresses and sermons during the preconvention Pastors' Conference.

From one point of view, and this is the way most of the state papers reported it at that time, Hobbs's address was a plea for the middle road, avoiding both extremes. The problem as I saw it then, and I see it now from this distant perspective, was the implication in that charged atmosphere that some were not adhering to the middle road. One part of the address, highly applauded, was a portion that allowed the audience to make its own conclusion as to the implied emphasis:

> It should be remembered, however, that this principle of unity in diversity imposes upon every Southern Baptist a sacred trust. The emphasis should be placed upon "unity," not "diversity." Liberty is no excuse for license. The greater body of Southern Baptists have always been a conservative people not given to extreme positions on theology, either on one side or the other. They have been, so to speak, a middle-of-the-road people.[82]

Shortly thereafter, two other portions of the address were received by the emotional crowd as an attack upon the seminaries in general and upon the author of *The Message of Genesis* in particular:

> Someone has described some of the current methods of teaching as the "shock" method designed to produce thought. This message may be used beneficially in theological education as in psychological therapy. But it should ever be remembered that the difference between shock therapy and an electrocution is the skill of the technician and the amount of electricity applied.[83]

This was followed by:

> Southern Baptists grant to their theologians freedom of investigation and thought. Indeed, they expect them to think ahead of them. But they expect them to think down the road by which they may follow, not in

---

[82]"President's Address," as reported in the *Arkansas Baptist*, 7 June 1962, 12.
[83]Ibid., 13.

the bypaths which lead to theological confusion.[84]

Perhaps these excerpts seem harmless enough in a calm setting. In the atmosphere of the day, however, it was another illustration of the disease of doublespeak which so easily implies whatever it is the hearer wants to hear. Whether the author so intended, only the author will know. However, as a shrewd strategist and skillful orator, Hobbs had been in similar kinds of situations many times before. In huge crowds, however, the demonic easily becomes operative and well-intentioned things can be distorted.

Particularly "biting" to me was the suggestion of the "shock treatment" teaching method. Especially in the field of New Testament studies, I felt I had been sometimes subjected to that technique in my own student days. Therefore, I spent long hours, often outside the classroom, trying to sustain a personal and devotional stance that would avoid such an approach. Therefore, although many greeted the speech with congratulatory relief, I received it with much pain.

One additional two-sentence section of Hobbs's address played directly into the hands of the severe critics. Whenever questions of Mosaic authorship or source criticism were discussed, literalists always responded with their belief that Jesus gave proof to the view of total Mosaic authorship. This had been debated back and forth across the denomination prior to San Francisco. The following sentences, in that context, were grist for the literalists' mill:

> The Old Testament must be interpreted in the light of the New Testament. Jesus Christ Himself is the final criterion of truth.[85]

Some, like the editor of the Tennessee Baptist state newspaper, could receive the words with commendations like "words of wise leadership" and "beware of both extremes."[86] The *Western Recorder* even spoke in glowing terms of "the Lord and a man" in commendation of Dr. Hobbs and his "masterpiece."[87] Most editors had the

---

[84]Ibid.
[85]Ibid., 14.
[86]Editorials, *Baptist and Reflector*, 7 June 1962, 4-5.
[87]"Daley Observations," *Western Recorder*, 21 June 1962, 4.

impression that Hobbs's address and his preaching placed the "conservatives" in the middle of the road against right-wing extremism. Editor Paul Allison, one of the antagonists in Kansas and editor of the Kansas *Baptist Digest,* understood the address as a description of "their" cause as conservative, but not right wing, and wrote, "We don't want to become a convention of right-wing rightists."[88] The convention as a whole received the president's address as an indication that the Oklahoma caucus people were "conservatives" (a sacred word), and not "right wingers." Thus, his contribution served to bless the critics' cause.

The way things moved shortly after the convention appeared to cause second thoughts, even for some who initially had experienced "congratulatory relief." Editor Chauncey Daley began to wonder whether the entire San Francisco episode did not indicate that "the minority could rule," and suggested that "some eastern states with large Baptist populations" were hardly represented in San Francisco. This ability by a certain segment meeting in a certain place to control a convention and the problem with improper credentials began to give him serious concern. According to Daley, "likely not half of the messengers at any Southern Baptist Convention has actually been approved by their local churches," and he was holding fears that the conventions would "become a Baptist mobocracy and resemble a political convention more than a meeting of God's people doing God's business."[89] Some felt that such was what happened at San Francisco; many are rather certain this prophetic fear has become real during the 1970s and 1980s.

Two themes surfaced in Hobbs's presidential address that did not attract much attention at the time but have since had great significance. He related the theme of the priesthood of the believer to both privilege and responsibility and cautioned that the responsibility aspect would lead personal viewpoints to need careful

---

[88]Allison, editorial: "We Had a Great Convention," *Baptist Digest,* 23 June 1962, 2.

[89]"The Minority Could Rule," in "Daley Observations," *Western Recorder,* 28 June 1962, 4-5.

evaluation.[90] Across the years this has been so twisted that in the 1988 meeting of the Southern Baptist Convention, the convention itself gave a mob vote so as to assure a collective control of the priesthood.

At the same time, I suppose because he felt some biblical interpretations had been ecumenically inspired, Hobbs cautioned the messengers against allowing undue ecumenical influence.[91] This bothered me at the time, but it came back to worry me even more as I reflected on it a few years later. Midwestern Seminary had excellent ecumenical relationships with other institutions in the Kansas City area. A professor from Central Baptist Seminary (American Baptist, in Kansas City, Kansas) and I had been instrumental in founding a theological society composed of faculty from Methodist, Roman Catholic, and other institutions in the larger Kansas City community. I do not know whether this had any part in triggering Hobbs's comments. It was, nevertheless, good preparation for me and helped to prepare me for my work as pastor of the Emmanuel Baptist Church in Albany, New York a few years later. This was the heyday of Vatican II and the ecumenical movement. Much of my work in Albany was ecumenical in nature. I taught on the faculties of three Roman institutions: St. Rose College, Siena College, and Our Lady of Angels Seminary. I likewise served on the Ecumenical Commission of the Roman Catholic Diocese of Albany and also helped to develop a continuing education program for the priests and nuns of the Catholic Diocese. This broad experience added to my Kansas City experience, helped me understand that to work ecumenically both deepens your own roots (through the necessity of knowing who you are) and enables one to share in witness and ministry to and with other groups, while sensing and appreciating the great commonality of experience shared by all Christians. It is an enriching opportunity.

In the midst of growing ecumenical relationships, I had cause to reflect on the negative ecumenical tones in Hobbs's convention address. Hobbs spoke on some occasion in my hometown of

---

[90]"President's Address," as reported in the *Arkansas Baptist*, 7 June 1962, 12.
[91]Ibid.

Danville, Virginia. Encountering one of my brothers there, Dr. Hobbs sent me greetings. I used that occasion as an opportunity to write to him and express my disappointment that he personally, so well equipped to make an ecumenical contribution and to lead Southern Baptists to do so, had instead confirmed their road of isolationism. Southern Baptists had an evangelism thrust that the ecumenical world so desperately needed, but the opportunity had been forfeited. Indeed, the nature of the San Francisco Convention had made Southern Baptists something of an enigma in the modern ecumenical world.

b. *Sunday School Board Activity.* No doubt viewing himself as reconciler and healer, Dr. Hobbs had "brokered" the convention. But James L. Sullivan of the Sunday School Board had also played a brokering role insofar as *The Message of Genesis* was concerned. The above-mentioned "congratulatory relief" had contributed to the solace of many of my extreme critics in that they felt they could not be accused of being "book-banners." I fear, however, that the motivation for refusing the ban was less than charitable.

Speaking editorially, Paul Allison of the *Baptist Digest* in Kansas gave insight to the strategy of those who were the political leaders against Midwestern when he suggested that "the book-banning motion, if passed, would have made a martyr of Dr. Elliott."[92] I never did feel like a martyr. Nevertheless, martyrdom publicity would perhaps have weakened the momentum of their cause. However, the book-banning refusal was only the "official" stance, as the unfolding episode of events will indicate.

The Sunday School Board had previously been scheduled to meet approximately one month after the San Francisco Convention, at which time it was to make an official and formal decision concerning the reprinting of *The Message of Genesis.* You will recall that Dr. Sullivan had made a "temporary" administrative decision about the matter, killing the book until such time as the Sunday School Board could meet. The conclusion of the meeting was somewhat set prior to the official meeting, judging from the promise

---

[92]Editorial: "We Had a Great Convention," *Baptist Digest,* 23 June 1962, 2.

of Dr. Sullivan at the convention in the conversation with Herschel Hobbs, Earl Harding, and Ralph Powell, when he indicated his fiat that the book not be reprinted.

Dr. Sullivan, prior to the July 1962 meeting, prepared a statement for the Plans and Policies Committee, the committee appointed by the Sunday School Board to make recommendations to the board on internal matters. In spite of the fact that the Sunday School Board had been very courageous in initially publishing the book and had defended its right to do so, there was now a depressed and changed atmosphere. The meeting of the convention had made a decided difference. Refusing outwardly to take any strong leadership on the question, Dr. Sullivan outlined six alternative actions which he suggested as possibilities for the board. Those six alternatives outlined in his Plans and Policies memo, "Concerning *The Message of Genesis* by Ralph Elliott," were these:

1. It might feel that the title should be continued as long as a sufficient number of orders are being received, and it might so instruct the administration to proceed with the printing as long as there is a market.
2. It can ask that the book not be reprinted at all, and publicize such decision widely.
3. It can ask that Dr. K. O. White, or someone else, write a book for publication setting forth a more conservative view to be studied along with the Elliott book.
4. It can ask the author to consider revisions before any reprints are authorized.
5. It can simply let the matter pass without taking any sort of action. In this event, the book will simply cease to be current. Since it is the feeling of the executive secretary that the title should not be reprinted by administrative decision, the book would neither be continued, nor banned, if the board takes no action. It would just not be in stock. Little or no publicity would or should be given if this route is taken.
6. It could take some other action which might seem more appropriate.

To this list of alternatives, Sullivan added, "I will gladly do what is deemed best when the majority of the board has expressed itself."[93]

At least two things are striking in these six options. First, absolutely no consideration appears to have been given to the contractual obligation to the author nor to the question of any of the legalities that might apply in the situation. There was still a legal, standing contract, but this was of less significance than the external pressures the board was facing. The integrity of a commitment by a denominational agency was of less importance than the desire to escape with the least possible criticism and culpability.

The other rather obvious matter is the evident weighting of his alternative number 5. Its presentation was designed both to get out of a jam and to escape the charge of book banning. It is interesting that the term "banned" is actually used in the explanation of the recommendation. Number 5 actually was Dr. Sullivan's recommendation, in spite of the fact that the contract with Broadman stated that the book was to be maintained in print as long as it was marketable. There was no question about the intent of the recommendation because Dr. Sullivan had indicated in his memorandum that the preconvention criticisms "created a strange effect, like that of a giant vacuum cleaner which almost suddenly sucked all the remaining copies out of the book stores and out of the warehouse. The editorial designed to oppose the book actually increased circulation. Back orders began to pile up in short order because no stock was on hand."[94] The acceptance of number 5 was a technical means of removing responsibility for the "banning" from all hands.

The Sullivan memo indicates that the "committee had already spent hundreds of man hours getting details and in making studies."[95] These "studies" clearly indicated which way the wind was blowing and the decision was made in accordance with the fifth alternative. Thus, Dr. Sullivan's administrative decision made in April 1962 remained in effect.

This "banning of the book by default" was looked upon by

---

[93]Sullivan, "Concerning *The Message of Genesis* by Ralph Elliott." This statement became public property when it was released in a circular memo Sullivan sent to "all Baptist state paper editors" and "all members of Sunday School Board of the Southern Convention," 7 August 1962.

[94]Ibid.

[95]Ibid.

many as less than an honest thing to do. Editor E. S. James of the Texas *Baptist Standard* was irate that the board did not have the stamina to declare forthrightly what it was doing. James, one of the most dogmatic of my critics, had spoken against Windham's motion at the convention upon the assurance that the Sunday School Board would handle the matter judiciously, and he did not consider such subterfuge judicious. It was in response to an editorial attack that Sullivan wrote to E. S. James his defensive letter of August 7, 1962, which was then circulated as a memorandum to all Baptist paper editors. James had written in his editorial that

> We cannot become enthusiastic about the passive manner with which the elected trustees accepted the suggestion. They simply voted to "let the matter pass without taking any sort of action." . . . this board's reaction seems to have been reluctant acquiescence.[96]

Sullivan sought to get off the hot seat by stating that:

> The motion before the Plans and Policies Committee that the board simply take no action was made by one of the most outstanding and dedicated Baptist pastors, who not only serves on the executive board of the Baptist General Convention of Texas but is also a member of the board of directors of the *Baptist Standard.* It is unthinkable that he would be any less careful in his denominational responsibilities when he is at the Sunday School Board than when he is dealing with *Baptist Standard* matters.[97]

Of course, what E. S. James had wanted was a board apology for allowing the book to be published in the first place; secondarily he wanted the board's apology for its January 1962 statement in which it defended its right to publish the book. James said, "If they were right in the January decision, then let them tell us why, for many of us think they were not."[98] In James's mind, there was something wrong with the Sunday School Board.

• • •

---

[96]James, "Sunday School Board Meeting Reviewed," *Baptist Standard,* 1 August 1962, 4.

[97]Sullivan, "Concerning *The Message of Genesis,* by Ralph Elliott."

[98]James, "Sunday School Board Meeting Reviewed," 4.

It is impossible to review the preconvention, convention, and postconvention actions regarding the book without realizing that Sullivan felt caught in the cross fire. Seeking to disentangle himself, Sullivan engaged in numerous conversations, and even made a convention conference promise not to allow the book to be reprinted. As mentioned earlier, this was what was told me by Herschel Hobbs. With regard to this, on July 27, 1962, Sullivan wrote to me that "no such agreement was contemplated or made at that time or at any other time with any person or group of persons."[99] I know of no way to resolve the discrepancy, but the dispute is quite illustrative of my primary remembrance of that particular period—scores of frightened convention personalities and functionaries frantically running in all directions for cover and for personal safety.

At any rate, when the action outlined above was communicated to me via the newspaper (as I recall, I never did receive any official communication from the Sunday School Board), I was deluged by the press who suggested that Sullivan had announced that steps would be taken "to return rights to the book to the author, who could seek another publisher." I replied that I assumed if they were willing to release the book, I would seek another publisher, and hoped that Broadman Press would be willing to help contact that publisher, which I saw as Broadman's responsibility. As a matter of fact, the editor and the general book editor of Broadman Press expressed genuine regret to me about the Sunday School Board's action and sought to be helpful in many ways, and against great obstacles.

Before I could give any thought to the future of the book, however, there were many remaining matters to be settled with regard to Midwestern Seminary, matters mandated by the San Francisco Convention.

---

[99]Sullivan, letter to the author, 27 July 1962.

# Chapter 5
# Confrontation and Dismissal

Long airplane flights can provide much opportunity for thought and reflection. There was much to think about on the flight from San Francisco to Kansas City. The geographical distance was the least of the journey. Hardly conscious of the physical flight itself, I took a long, reflective journey into the corridors of my soul.

There was no great sense of fear about the uncertainties that lay ahead. There was some anxiety over the lack of clarity about the implications of the actions taken by the convention. I saw a road not yet traveled, but assumed it would be a somewhat difficult way as the trustees of Midwestern Seminary would seek to clarify for themselves the implications of the San Francisco mandate.

I was physically, mentally, and emotionally tired from the convention ordeal, yet more immediately concerned on the Saturday flight to Kansas City that I had to preach the next morning at Calvary Baptist Church where I was a member and for some eighteen months had served as interim pastor. It would be late when I arrived in Kansas City, and there would be little additional time for Sunday preparation. How would I be received at the church after the much-publicized furor in San Francisco? I was much more anxious about facing my church on the morrow than about any later confrontation with the trustees.

Those immediate anxieties, however, proved unfounded. The embrace of that local church gave me a strength that sustained me through the confrontation and dismissal to come. I have had enough firsthand encounters with local churches to know that, like all institutions, even the local church is often diseased and needs constantly to be reborn. Nevertheless, the experience with that one local church at such a needy time in my life has convinced me that at all times the local church, even with its imperfections, is a genuine expression of the Body of Christ, without which human existence for me would be impossible.

Since many of my critics accused me of not believing in God, Christ, or church, it is worthwhile to describe what happened when I returned from the convention. As the plane neared touchdown, I found myself breathing hard, fearing that my church colleagues probably felt I had become a disgrace. Several news releases had indicated I was serving as interim pastor at Calvary. I assumed the church would resent such a connection that might damage the church's image in the conservative Missouri environment. My worries proved to be needless.

As I stepped from the plane at the downtown Kansas City airport, I could scarcely believe what I saw: 200 or more people from Calvary Baptist Church were gathered at the foot of the exit stairway. They had come to assure me of their affection and support. It was a tremendous emotional boost, and I could only respond with tears of thanksgiving.

Much earlier than necessary the next morning, I went to the church study to try to prepare myself to lead in morning worship. It was a quiet and reflective time until there was a knock at the door, and the chairman of deacons came in. His greeting was brief and his words were few. He said that all the deacons wished to meet with me before the morning worship. He went on to tell me the deacons had met earlier, and that there were some things they needed to share with me. My heart sank, and the fears returned. By now, I had come to expect the worst when anyone asked to speak to me about anything.

Some fifteen minutes before the service, there was a second knock, and this distinguished group of people, the entire board of deacons, silently filed into the room. Their appointed spokesperson said something like, "We know you are going through a lot, and we don't understand it all, but we want you to know that we know you, and we believe in you, and we are with you!" They moved out with reverence to allow me to recover.

Seldom have I known such grace, and seldom have I felt so

humbled by such a community of love. The worship service was just ahead, and I entered it with confidence—and it happened again. It was yet in those days when church attendance was large. That morning the place was packed, all seats taken on both the main level and in the balcony. As the associate minister and I walked into the chancel area, everyone stood in support. Once more, I was so overwhelmed as to find it difficult for the next step. Our services were broadcast on radio in those days, and punctuality was important, so I whispered to the associate minister to take my part of the liturgy and get us started. When it came time to preach, I was ready. I will never forget the occasion. There was such prayerful support that I knew the Word was enfleshed in a new way and that the sacrament of preaching was real. Since those days, my interest in Dietrich Bonhoeffer has sent me around the world lecturing on *Sanctorum communio* ("Communion of Saints") and other things, but nothing has done more to strengthen my understanding of and commitment to the covenanted community of faith than my experiences with Calvary Baptist Church, both in its collective and many individual expressions.

The support continued, but my own euphoria was somewhat moderated by the difficult sequence of events from July to October of that year. Having been encouraged by San Francisco, the critics were determined to keep the momentum going until they accomplished their purposes.

## The Immediate Issues

The immediate issues ostensibly were two: what to do about the book, and what to do about the San Francisco resolution, passed *instead* of the book-banning one, and stating that

[O]ur institutions and other agencies [are to] take such steps as shall be necessary to remedy at once those situations where such views now threaten our historic position.

The July 12-13 action of the Sunday School Board to prevent the reprinting of the book, by default, has been reported. What I have not previously reported is the disappointment of the editors of Broadman Press, William J. Fallis and Joseph F. Green, Jr. Almost immediately (the first letter I can find is dated July 25, 1962), William Fallis began, on my behalf, to seek another publisher and suggested that the plates of the book could be transferred for that purpose. (Perhaps not until this present moment have I sensed the agony these men must have experienced and the risks they took in my behalf. Belatedly, I seek to express my profound gratitude.)

By August 1962, Dr. Fallis was suggesting a formal contract to transfer the plates and the copyright to me so that the book might be reissued by another publisher.[1] The hysteria about the book continued. (Fallis discovered that his own son had hid the book under his mattress and was reading it during the night!) The fate of the book, however, is connected with the matter of the continuing concern and action of the seminary trustees.

Shortly after the San Francisco convention and resolution, Malcolm Knight, then pastor of Southside Baptist Church in Jacksonville, Florida, and president of the Midwestern trustees, announced there would be a special meeting of the trustees "to try to determine just what the convention at San Francisco did say, and to make plans to carry that out."[2]

In my own mind, there was no uncertainty as to what the resolution said or meant. It meant my days were numbered. Some of the trustees, however, appeared to pretend they were in a quandary as to what it meant; two or three honestly felt there was some other way to satisfy the mandate of the resolution, and so there was a modicum of hope in the air.

At that time, Herschel Hobbs, the president of the convention, began to become more directly involved in resolving the affair. Malcolm Knight reportedly wrote to Dr. Hobbs on June 30, 1962 and requested his interpretation of the action. Hobbs made it clear to Jackson that the trustees had to "take whatever steps may be necessary to comply with the actions of the convention."[3]

---

[1]Fallis, letter to the author, 21 August 1962.

[2]See Gainer E. Bryan, Jr., "Knight Outlines Plan of Seminary Trustees," *The Maryland Baptist*, 26 July 1962, 2.

[3]Hobbs, correspondence to Knight, 16 July 1962, as reported by Sally Rice, "Ralph Elliott: Controversial Figure among Southern Baptist," a paper submitted to the Duke University Department of Religion, 15 April 1963, 51.

Subsequent movements on the part of Dr. Hobbs suggested to me that he understood this to mean that the primary task of the Midwestern trustees was to deal with me.

Personally, I feel that President Berquist and others began to weaken in their determination when Hobbs injected himself into the picture. About this time, Hobbs made visits to Trustee Robert Jackson and several others. In turn, Bob Jackson, President Berquist, and a third party whose identity now eludes me—I think it was Malcolm Knight—took me to a "pressure" luncheon at the Hereford House in Kansas City. Often during that luncheon, the repartee (not so witty as the word implies) was, "But Herschel says. . . ." This suggested capitulation to Hobbs's wishes.

At some point prior to September, Dr. Hobbs visited Kansas City for a top-level conference with Dr. Knight and Dr. Berquist. I was called into the conference and questioned quite extensively by Dr. Hobbs and Dr. Knight. On another occasion, President Berquist reported he had received a telephone call from Dr. Hobbs requesting that Berquist ask me to disown the book. At any rate, these and other pressures led to a meeting of the trustees' Executive Committee on July 31, 1962. The result of this was a call for a special meeting of the full board of trustees to be held September 27-28.

There was little question as to what was likely to happen at the September meeting. Already, on July 20, I had written to a friend in England and suggested:

> At that time I will be tried again for the same "crime" for which I have already been tried and acquitted. This time it is going to be even more difficult, for the organized opposition was most successful in stacking our board of trustees. In addition, they are working hard to unseat Dr. Berquist. I frankly do not see how I can survive again. I think the other men will be safe for the time being, but it will only be a matter of time before they tackle Peacock, and then Morton, and then Ashcraft, in that order. Thus, though I feel obligated to stay through the board meeting, I also feel that I need a place to land.
>
> It is one thing to be dismissed for personality problems with the administration; it is something else to be dismissed for supposed heresy. I would very much like to teach, for I feel that my life is committed in that direction. Even a department of religion in a state

university would be challenging, for there I could at least help to salvage the faith and lives of so many young people who are caught in the quandary of our present generation. I very much enjoy preaching, and for the last five months have been interim pastor at the Calvary Baptist Church here in Kansas City. I could have gone to Calvary, from all indications, but I insisted that they look elsewhere. I have done so because I do not feel that it would be best for the church to have me since I have been so closely identified with the seminary, and I feel that it would be best for me to get out of this immediate environment in the event that I have to go. Calvary has been wonderful to me in putting her arms of fellowship around us during this particular time.[4]

I have quoted extensively from this letter because it indicates something of the climate at the time and verifies what I have often said, namely, that the October 1962 dismissal by the trustees was anticlimactic.

Between July and September, the entire faculty was caught in the struggle, and for the most part, with genuine concern for me, shared their counsel and advice along with their friendship and prayerful support. I think the reason for this was their honest caring for me, but also the realization of an even larger issue at stake: the question of the nature and purpose of theological education itself. One of the faculty members in particular was almost one hundred percent accurate in what he predicted would happen when he wrote:

> You are going to be told that only your resignation will save the school. You are going to be told that if you leave, Dr. Berquist and the rest of us remain. They are going to try to put on your back and conscience the burden of the destruction which they are bringing about.
> . . . I would guess that some trustee will work behind the scene to divide you and Dr. Berquist so as to make it appear that your going would save him, but your insistence to remain would ruin him.[5]

Those words were written on August 24, 1962. History has proved them to have been an accurate prediction. Events developed almost as written.

---

[4]Elliott, letter to Dale Moody, 20 July 1962.
[5]Morris Ashcraft, letter to the author, 24 August 1962.

During August, the faculty discussed the impact the turmoil was likely to have on the school's future, and pondered how all might best prepare for the September board meeting. On August 28, the faculty hammered out a long statement and mailed it to every Baptist state paper, affirming that "we do believe that the biblical revelation is relevant and authoritative for our day." Looking back, that appears to have been a very neutral and safe statement. Little was accomplished by it.

In the meanwhile, the air was filled with all kinds of rumors regarding preparations for the September board meeting. The disgruntled Missouri group, the leaders of the initial Oklahoma caucus, those trustees who had moved from Central Seminary to help establish Midwestern but who did not secure desired positions, were very busy. There were leaked telephone conversations that indicated a plan to place everyone at the seminary on probation. If the antagonists did not get their way, they would accuse the president and the vice president of the mismanagement of funds and of favoritism in building bids and contract commitments. One of the leaders complained that he had not been consulted about the employment of the campus architect.[6] The closer we got to September, the more the pressure, the more ruthless the tactics, and the more certain that initially *The Message of Genesis* was only a small part of the original plan of the Missouri group.

## The September Board Meeting

The two issues, the book banning and the San Francisco resolution, came together at the September 27-28 board meeting.

### 1. The Full Board

Those who had engineered things in San Francisco were certain that the unspecified action indicated in the convention resolution meant to fire Ralph Elliott. That action would also be a chastisement of Millard Berquist whom by now they had come thoroughly to dislike. Therefore, when the board met, the critics aggressively

---

[6]Priveleged correspondence in the author's files.

moved "to instruct the president of Midwestern to obtain the immediate resignation of Dr. Ralph Elliott from the faculty of Midwestern." This would both embarrass the president and take care of the culprit whom they had by now portrayed as one whose viewpoints were totally destructive to the Scriptures.

In an unanticipated parliamentary procedure, the chair of the board ruled that the motion in essence was a motion for dismissal and that such a motion would require a two-thirds vote to carry. His ruling was appealed, but the appeal lost by one vote. An impasse took place because the maker of the motion and his supporters either could not or would not place a formal charge against me in order to float a motion for dismissal. The impasse was resolved by a motion to table.

## 2. A Special Committee

Since twenty votes, the number required for dismissal, did not for the time seem available, a special committee was authorized to meet with me and to come back with a solution. On September 28, I met with the committee for approximately four and one-half hours. Mutually, we sought to work out a statement that might resolve our difficulties. We were together on statements of concern and regret with reference to the furor in the convention. With tablet in hand, the following material was devised in a give-and-take discussion. I scribbled furiously, but the wording is approximate, since there was writing and rewriting during the period of the discussion itself:

> We recognize that the literary, critical, and historical approach to the Scriptures is a valid approach to biblical study. This must not be an end in itself, but directed towards an emphasis of a positive nature in nurturing and deepening faith. Such demands that the professor seek to ascertain where the student is and make an effort to graduate instruction to his needs. The presentation of this method is questioned by some Baptists. Our professors are called upon to present the material in such a way as to allow the student to reach his own conclusions without ridicule or prejudice. With reference to the conclusions reached through this method, some are tentative and some are conclusive. An effort must be made by the professor to distinguish between tentative and positive conclusions.

In the immediate problem of *The Message of Genesis*, the author admits that many of his conclusions are tentative and subject to change. The author further recognizes that people may reach different conclusions. Of conclusions reached and worded, it may be said that the author feels that some could be improved upon. When a conclusion has been reached by the author, this is no denial of the possibility of God having worked another way.

Although the author and professor reaffirms his commitment to the basic approach expressed in the book, he recognizes the necessity of continually living with spiritual and intellectual repentance, with the end result of his ministry being a contribution to the authority of the Bible and the evangelistic proclamation of the Gospel. The author regrets that the impression has been left that this is not his concern and he regrets the convention crisis which has partially resulted therefrom, and will seek to give more careful expression of word, both taught and written.[7]

## The October Investigating Committee

Although every person on the committee contributed something to this statement, no formal vote was taken, for near the end of the meeting (and this helped to bring the meeting to an end), Trustee Morgan of Texas suggested that this still did not handle the book, nor could he, after giving it thought, agree to the first part. Thus, the committee reported to the full board that more time was needed. Time was granted, and the committee was scheduled to meet again on October 17-18.

Chairman Malcolm Knight asked me to make myself available for a further meeting with the committee on October 17 at 4:00 p.m. I was available, but was not asked by the committee to appear until 11:00 a.m. on October 18.

The October 18 meeting was opened by a statement from Chairman Knight that they were not satisfied with the teaching and writing that had come from me. He stated that the committee had unanimously agreed on nine points to which I was to give either a

---

[7]I have the scribbled, marked, remarked, and marked-out notes from this meeting in my files.

negative or positive response. This represented a different direction, for in the previous committee meeting, we worked on the project together. However, I responded to each of the points, after which there was questioning, elaboration, and discussion. The nine points were not unlike the material worked on at the September 28 committee meeting, and I found it possible to give my support. Once more, it appeared that "we might make it," but then, as a last factor, the committee asked whether I would "volunteer" not to seek the republication of the book. I responded that this did not seem the proper action for me to take, but that I would like some time to think it over. I was troubled by the suggestion that volunteering to suppress the book might suggest I had changed my mind on the matters in the book. This would enable me to return to the classroom. The time was late afternoon. I was given until 7:00 that evening to reflect on the matter.

I left the hotel where we were meeting and went home to talk with my wife and to think things over. I felt I had reached a decision, but wanted to talk with others to see whether my thinking was sound or whether I was being too subjective. Three of my seminary colleagues, Professors Ashcraft, Honeycutt, and Peacock, came to my home to help me with that analysis. I was certain in my own mind as to what I needed to do. I was held back only by my concern that my wife Virginia understand the gravity of the situation. When she said, "Ralph, if you go down there and sell your soul, don't come home," I knew we were together, and it was easy to do what I had to do.

When I returned to the hotel, I indicated that after conscientious reflection, I could not volunteer to deny the book's republication should occasion for republication arise. I felt that withdrawal of the book, in addition to things I have already suggested, would deny the basic freedom on which Christian community is built, and that it would likewise create an atmosphere of fear and tension that would impose limitations both in the classroom and in projects of writing and research.

After I shared my decision and its justification, Chairman Malcolm Knight addressed me with a new proposal. How would I react if the full board voted to request me to no longer seek republication. I replied that if the committee reported to the board that the committee felt that I had made an error in judgment, and therefore recommended to the board that the board request me to withhold the book, I would willingly accede to the request of the board. Someone asked whether I would do this with a good spirit, and I said "Yes." Trustee Humphreys of Kentucky and Trustee McCrummen of Alabama spoke up and said they had learned enough about me to affirm that this would be true.

Trustee Curry of Missouri suggested that we seemed to have a happy solution, and moved to go into executive session to consider the matter. I was asked to leave the meeting room. There seemed to be a general consensus that the proposal was a good one. I felt it was something I could live with as long as I was an employee of Midwestern. The difference between "volunteering" to do something and "acceding if ordered as an employee" might seem a small point for some, but in my mind at that time, it was a difference that enabled me to live with dignity and integrity. As I was leaving the room, however, I suddenly realized that it was not likely to succeed because I heard Trustee Earl Harding mutter that he did not want the responsibility of banning the book.

I left the committee and was never called back again, although I was instructed to remain at the hotel, and did so until after midnight. Since I had not been allowed to have any counsel with me during any of the deliberations and now felt very much alone, I asked my three faculty colleagues mentioned above to come and sit with me while I waited. Since the committee had not been in executive session until that point, I felt free to discuss with my colleagues what had happened thus far. At some point in the evening, the committee took a brief recess, and Dr. Knight came out to speak with me. He was very much disturbed to see that my three faculty friends were with me and nervously emphasized that I had no right to discuss the affairs with anyone since everything was considered executive session. This appeared strange to me since the group voted to go into executive session only as I left the room. I felt this to be a strong reprimand and the emphasis on silence unjust. Nevertheless, it was evident that the presence of my friends was not well received, so I asked them to leave the hotel and return home. I recall having thought at the moment of "brainwashing" and "Gestapo tactics," quite an approach for servants of the church.

During that brief encounter with Malcolm Knight, I did get some inkling that Earl Harding and his supporters were carrying the meeting, and that pressure was being placed on President Berquist of having the onus of ordering me to withhold the book, rather than having the trustees bear that burden. I finally left the hotel after midnight without any further contact. I assumed the next crisis would be at the meeting of the full board of trustees which had been called for November 29-30.

## The Dismissal Meeting

It was quite clear what the next step would mean. For that reason, the next morning at the breakfast table my wife decided to share the word with our two children, Jenny and Bev, then ages eight and ten. She told them we would be moving because the seminary wanted me to do something that I could not do.

Events moved even more swiftly than I had imagined. Before leaving the Muehlbach Hotel meeting, the investigative committee called for a full board meeting on October 25-26, much earlier than the November 29-30 date previously announced. They did this with no announcement or notice to me or inquiry as to whether I could be present. Although Dr. Berquist and I had talked in late afternoon October 19, no mention was made of the new date.

I was scheduled that week to be in Virginia to preach at a revival meeting. Dr. Malcolm Knight finally called me in Virginia and said it was an oversight that I had not been notified, and asked me to be present at the October 25-26 meeting. So it was necessary for me to fly back to Kansas City on those dates to receive my dismissal notice from the trustees.

Having been formally dismissed, I returned to Virginia and completed the revival meeting. Needless to say, I was myself not very much revived.

## Some Dismissal Reflections

During the October 25 meeting, the trustees were reminded, in writing, of my previous statement:

> Since the board of trustees feels that the Convention would better be served by not republishing the book, I acquiesce in the request of the trustees that *The Message of Genesis* not be republished.

The statement was completely ignored, however, because by this time the trustees had decided to try to protect themselves against any possible charges of book banning. I had, by the way, on October 20 written a special letter to Board Chairman Malcolm Knight as a reminder because it already had become obvious to me that things were going to go another way. I was much disturbed that in the trustee announcement of the October 25 dismissal no mention was made of the acquiescence, and it was made to appear that I stubbornly resisted the call of my president and therefore had to be removed because of insubordination. The trustees had succeeded, not only in making scapegoats of both Dr. Berquist and me, but likewise of driving a piercing stake into the heart of a great friendship. The trustees had accomplished the ban, but hoped they had escaped the blame. At any rate, I concur with these words written by someone else:

> [I]t is incredible that Elliott was dismissed for refusing to do what the Southern Baptist Convention had refused to do in June, the Sunday School Board had refused to do in July, and Midwestern's board of trustees had refused to do in September. They all refused to ban the book, but Elliott was dismissed because he refused to.[8]

Regardless of what the trustees thought their reasons to be, their action was a violation of all acceptable academic standards used as

---

[8]Morris Ashcraft, professor of theology at Midwestern Seminary, memo to a closed group of personal friends entitled "A Report on the Elliott Controversy," 21 November 1962, 6.

a guide for educational institutions.[9] All Baptist professors were placed under threat. That threat has increased across the years, and professors in every Southern Baptist seminary have lost any sense of liberty and freedom. No guideline is sufficiently strong to offer protection, as was discovered in that early era when trustees totally ignored the Articles of Faith previously placed in the seminary's bylaws for this kind of an event. At that time, my faculty colleague asked, "Does that mean that the politicians will control *all* aspects of denominational life?"[10] The passage of time has answered the question with a resounding "Yes!"

Strangely, during these events the secular press was at times more perceptive, or at least more free, than was the religious press. Even the *New York Post* could express its concern on its editorial page:

> It is not only under communism that the claims of reason and intellect are challenged by authoritarianism and the scholar ordered to subordinate objectivity and the rules of evidence to "higher" considerations.
>
> In Kansas City, Dr. Ralph H. Elliott has been dismissed from the faculty of Midwestern Theological Seminary because his book on "The Message of Genesis" treated the biblical account of creation as symbolic and theological rather than literal and historical.
>
> The pressures against free inquiry in the U.S. are of a minor order of magnitude as compared with those under communism. But the appeal of authoritarianism is universal, as the Elliott case in Kansas City suggests, and the battle for freedom of conscience must be unceasing.[11]

---

[9]Cf. "Concerning the Elliott Controversy," *Baptists for Freedom* (February 1963) 6.

[10]Ashcraft, "A Report on the Elliott Controversy."

[11]*New York Post*, 29 October 1962, editorial.

Chapter 6

# The Odyssey
# of a Book's Reprinting

Whether *The Message of Genesis* should or should not be reprinted was often a focal point of the discussions from July to October 1962, but the reprinting of the book was not the primary issue. An editorial in *The Christian Century*, "The Desecration of Liberty," understood the basic issue then and what it was to be for the future.

> The issue is not heresy or the right of a professor to teach such mild biblical criticism. The issue is a much more vast one: control of the Southern Baptist Convention's academic institutions and, through this, of the training of the ministry. The theological reactionaries in the convention are determined to wrest control of the convention's institutions from the hands of those academic and theological leaders who respect the truth concerning the Bible and are determined to maintain respectable academic standards in their denomination's seminaries and colleges. The dismissal of Professor Elliott is bad news . . . for the faculties and students of other schools of the denomination. It is a warning that they will have a fight on their hands if they want to preserve academic freedom, intellectual integrity, and creditable scholarship in the institutions they love and serve. It is bad news for the Southern Baptist Convention, whose unity is now gravely imperiled by a desecration of the religious liberty whose defense is the special pride of Baptists.[1]

The thesis stated in this editorial is exactly what moderate Southern Baptists are struggling with today. It is a liberty that for the most

---

[1]*The Christian Century*, 14 November 1962, 1376.

part has been lost.

The point is that we were grappling with larger issues, issues that would affect the future. The book was but a symbol of the larger issue. Nevertheless, symbols are important, and the time came after the dismissal to give the symbol some attention to see whether it might be kept alive.

The book was of minimal importance compared with the larger issues. My time was absolutely limited by my total expenditure of energies in keeping up with day to day political events. But I also put off attention to reprinting because I seriously doubted any other publisher would wish to reprint the book. The book may have been too liberal for some, but it was too conservative for many others. When interviewed by Baptist Press on October 29, 1962, I suggested that "I think the possibility of republishing the book is most remote because it is slanted toward Southern Baptists and is not stiff enough for other groups."[2]

So far as I can determine, the first inkling that the book might *not* be reprinted by Broadman Press was in a July 6, 1962 letter from William J. Fallis, Broadman book editor, prior to the meeting of the Sunday School Board that followed the San Francisco Convention. Fallis wrote:

> I do not see how we can afford to discontinue publication of the book. To do so would really negate convention action in refusing to ban it, but some people are trying to decide the issue for us.[3]

I think I realized then that the book was probably doomed at Broadman. Fallis was a very supportive friend, however, and I began to consider the possibility of its being placed somewhere else by what he said in his letter of 25 July:

> I have been in touch with one denominational publisher and have made an official approach to. . . . I should like to wait until we can get something worked out on a new publisher before writing anything

---

[2]Donald J. Sorensen, "Elliott Feels He Made a Concession," *Baptist Press*, 29 October 1962, 2.

[3]Fallis, letter to the author, 6 July 1962.

definite about canceling the contract.[4]

By August 1962, Dr. Fallis had concluded that circumstances made it difficult for him to do much more. He continued to encourage me to place the book elsewhere, and sent me a list of prospective publishers.[5] Shortly thereafter, he indicated that "the transfer of proofs or plates can be handled when you have secured another publisher."[6]

After the Midwestern board of trustees September 1962 meeting, I apparently had reached the conclusion that although the reprinting of the book by anyone was unlikely, and that indeed the book was a minor note in the total scenario, I should nonetheless close out my relationship with Broadman Press. I therefore wrote to Bill Fallis on October 2 that

> It seems that time has come to do something in a definite way relative to concluding any publishing agreement. . . . I think the committee which was appointed (September) agrees that the issue is neither the book nor a person, but the validity of a particular approach, as one approach, to Old Testament studies in a Southern Baptist institution. . . . I am beginning to doubt that anyone else will desire to publish the book until my status here is cleared. It occurs to me that most publishers would not desire to publish such a book by a person who is no longer connected with an educational institution. Thus, if something fruitful should turn up in the way of publishing the book at a later date, then I suppose the transfer of proofs or plates will have to be handled as a specific instance by itself.[7]

My motivation and interest in reprinting was developing, but I did not send out letters of inquiry to various publishers until October 9, 1962. In those letters, I indicated that "the type can be obtained from Broadman," for this was my understanding based on earlier telephone conversations and Fallis's letter of August 21.

D. L. Duxbury, a pastor friend in Kansas City, took it upon

---

[4]Fallis, letter to the author, 25 July 1962.
[5]Fallis, letter to the author, 14 August 1962.
[6]Fallis, letter to the author, 21 August 1962.
[7]My letter to Fallis, 2 October 1962.

himself to initiate a telephone inquiry to Darrell K. Wolfe, director of the Bethany Press, publishing arm of the Christian Board of Publication of the Disciples of Christ. On November 8, 1962, Mr. Wolfe wrote to me that they wanted to publish the book, and on the same date he wrote to Bill Fallis to request that Broadman ship the type to them. On November 12, 1962, I signed an acceptance with Broadman Press, releasing me from my relationship with that publisher. On the 13th of November, I gave final approval to Bethany Press and severed negotiations with two other publishers who had indicated an interest in the book.

Immediately following Darrell Wolfe's November 8 letter requesting the type from Broadman, we began to run into trouble. Mr. Wolfe telephoned to tell me that Broadman had indicated the type was not standing, that 200 trays of lead type had been melted, that therefore the type was not available to send to Bethany. There was a flurry of telephone calls back and forth to various people at the Sunday School Board in Nashville. It was the only time in all the tangled relationships during the so-called "Genesis controversy" that I felt I would finally have to seek legal counsel. Ultimately legal counsel was not necessary, and I was extremely pleased that it was not. I had strong personal disinclination (even moral concerns) about legal action against any person or organization within the community of faith.

I had to conclude that someone at the Southern Baptist Sunday School Board was deliberately seeking to block the reprinting of the book. Although they were not contractually involved anymore, they apparently felt that the best way to keep unwanted attention and publicity away from themselves was to just let the book die. The stalemate did not begin to break until Bethany indicated that since the type was not available, they would photograph the book and produce it in that manner. When Broadman discovered that Bethany was determined, with or without type, the type suddenly became available again.

I do not wish to place any responsibility upon Dr. Fallis because he had sought always to be helpful, and I suspect at times at risk to himself. He could only respond on the basis of information given him, but on December 6, 1962, I received from him the following message:

> I had been told that the type had been killed, but later we discovered that the printer had not yet destroyed the type. He had asked for clearance to do so because he needed the lead and knew that we would not be reprinting the book. The type *is* still standing in the shop, and we are awaiting further word from Bethany Press.[8]

Nevertheless, the logjam did not finally break until December 17, 1962 after Darrell K. Wolfe wrote a rather hard-nosed inquiry:

> Needless to say, Bill, I think there has been a very unnecessary delay on the part of Broadman Press, and it looks seriously to me as though Broadman Press would rather not sell us the type. What do you say about it?[9]

The book was finally published again in February 1963, received rather popular support, and stayed in print and circulation for about twenty years before normal attrition led to its demise.

---

[8]Fallis, letter to the author, 6 December 1962.
[9]Wolfe, letter to Fallis, 17 December 1962.

# Chapter 7

# Some Personal Reflections

At Gorbachev's press conference following the failed coup, a young woman from *Newsweek* asked Mr. Gorbachev what he had learned from his seventy-two-hour crisis which put him in isolation from the country at large. It was perhaps too early for him to attempt to answer that question because such answers come only by reflective trial and error over a long period of time. I continue to struggle with some of the questions of the "Genesis controversy" these many years later. Because it was, I believe, the initiation of an effort within the Southern Baptist Convention that has finally reached ascendancy during the last decade, it is an issue that shall remain with me all of my life. When on occasion it has become dormant and or of only peripheral focus, something has happened to bring it back to center. The "Genesis controversy," I thus conclude, involved some of the basic ingredients that are part of a systemic order in institutional religion.

## The Cause of the Struggle

Why did it happen? Throughout this narrative I have affirmed my belief that some ambitious but disappointed people were dealing with a hunger for personal power. But I believe there was and is a deeper element. It has to do with the nature of theological education and the purpose of seminary or divinity school training. Is it education or indoctrination? Is it thesis or praxis? Is it head or heart? Is it spiritual formation or intellectual acquisition?

It is rather strange to me that those were the issues in my own mind as the handful of us who established Midwestern Seminary tried to provide shape and purpose for the new school. And these are the questions that recently have been at the heart of the pastoral-theology movement. Edward Farley, Joseph C. Hough, Jr., Max Stackhouse, James Poling, Don Browning, and many more, continue to raise tough questions about the nature and purposes of theological education.[1] During my two years of service as provost at Colgate Rochester Divinity School/Bexley Hall/Crozer Theological Seminary, one of my major tasks was curriculum review and reform, and I was faced again with the same basic questions of those early seminary years. It has been a lifetime question.

## 1. The Early Years

I began my work at Midwestern with this basic question, and I ended my work there with the question still before me. Portions of my academic address (the first given at the new seminary, since I was the first professor to be installed) were devoted to the issue. Shortly after I was dismissed, I received a letter from Heber Peacock, chair of the program committee of the Midwestern Faculty Club, who was preparing for a January 14, 1963 presentation on this very issue. In part, his letter read:

> The Program Committee of the Faculty Club has agreed that we would like for you to address us on January 14, 1963, as originally scheduled. . . . We would appreciate very much your willingness to come and address us on the subject of "Theological Education and Seminary Structure." The events which have occurred do not alter your keen insights into the problems . . . related to curriculum and interstructure. . . . I wish you would say to us some of the things about interrelatedness of departments which you gave to the Kansas City Theological Society.[2]

Actually, some of my concerns were similar to the concerns of some of my critics. We might have been able to accomplish something together had we been able to hear each other. Gorbachev would have benefited much and the entire cause of democratization

---

[1]Edward Farley, *Theologia: The Fragmentation and Unity of Theological Education* (Philadelphia: Fortress Press, 1983) has provided the most stringent recent stimulus.

[2]Peacock, letter to the author, 12 November 1962.

would have been much further along had he been able to hear Boris Yeltsen six months prior to the attempted Soviet coup. Perhaps some alliances might have been formed with a different ending had the Baptist "hardliners" realized that I felt that some of their concerns were legitimate concerns. Let me quote from the academic address I gave in 1960 shortly after we moved onto the new campus:

> But let it be emphasized from the beginning that the Discipline of Old Testament Language cannot be considered in isolation, removed from other areas of theological interest. Already too long, seminary education has been the pursuit of various subjects, with seldom an opportunity provided for cross-fertilization of thought and interest. Far too often the seminarian has graduated with a multiplicity of courses under his intellectual belt, yet having had, not once, an opportunity to pull the subject matter together by being forced to ask, "How does THIS relate to THAT?" . . . Such compartmentalized education has led to a segregated concept of the Bible. . . . The very structure of seminary life into Old Testament and New Testament departments may be psychologically responsible.[3]

This emphasis was continued with several other corollaries such as involve Bible study and sermon preparation, church thought and church action. I especially emphasized "going beyond higher criticism" in order to ask the "so-what" questions. "The academic study of the Old Testament," I said, "always has as its ultimate goal the clarification of the *meaning* of God's word and work." I concluded with the sentence, "The direction in our Old Testament study must be a wedding of head and heart!"[4]

The address was directed towards Old Testament study, but that specific in the general setting of the seminary included by inference all areas of theological study.

---

[3]From the original manuscript, in my possession.
[4]Ibid.

## 2. The In-Between Years

Since I began and ended my life's work in a seminary faculty setting,[5] I often refer to my many years in the pastoral setting as the "in-between years." They were wonderful years, but my concerns remained much the same: How does one relate thesis and praxis? This was the focal point of a considerable amount of debate in American Baptist life when I promoted again the joining of head and heart in championing "the minister as professional."[6] In my treatment of the subject, I used "profession" in its root ecclesiastical sense of "call to excellence" and undergirded the various kinds of calls as they were originally enunciated by H. Richard Niebuhr and tested in practice by Jack D. Glasse.[7]

## 3. The Later Years

Although I must discount wholesome motives for the leaders of the attack against Midwestern Seminary, I believe many, if not most, of the people caught up in the hysteria of that effort had a genuine concern for the maintenance of those things that are normative for the church and for its practical expression in the life of the people and in the world. The careful strategizing by the seminary's enemies was so successful that multitudes were convinced that sacred things had been irreverently considered. In their minds, the teaching office of the church was being desecrated. There was intense concern for the teaching, preaching, and pastoral care offices of the church. Today, people are writing books directed towards

---

[5]My last position before retirement was first as provost, then as vice president for academic life and dean of faculty at Colgate Rochester Divinity School/Bexley Hall/Crozer Theological Seminary.

[6]Cf. Ralph H. Elliott, "The Minister as Professional," *Foundations* 22 (April-June 1979) 116-24.

[7]The following older books are very helpful. H. Richard Niebuhr, *The Purpose of the Church and Its Ministry* (New York: Harper & Row Publishers, 1956); Charles William Stewart, *Person and Profession* (Nashville: Abingdon Press, 1974); and James D. Glasse, *Profession: Minister* (Nashville: Abingdon Press, 1968).

reclaiming these offices.[8] If such energies had been directed constructively rather than destructively, it is possible some areas of the church would be stronger today. As it is, we still struggle to reclaim some things that were lost or minimized.

When we were engaged in serious curriculum review at Colgate Rochester Divinity School, I wrote to hundreds of people—Episcopal bishops and American Baptist executive ministers, pastors, lay leaders, and a large variety of people—asking basically one question: Knowing what you know about the life and mission of the church, if you were responsible for a curriculum to train ministers, what would that curriculum look like? There was a sizable response, and in nearly every instance a request for a balance between thesis and praxis and an undergirding of interdisciplinary relationships. Stereotypes did not hold. In other words, one cannot say that Episcopalians asked for *this* and Baptists asked for *that*. Both Episcopal bishops and Baptist executive ministers asked that the classical disciplines of Bible, theology, church history, and ministry continue to be in focus, but in the context of preaching, knowing how to teach and share the Scriptures, spirituality, personal relationships, administration, stewardship, and conflict resolution.

In those early days, I was trying to do the biblical work around the theme of biblical covenant and an understanding of covenant community so that the various practical expressions of the church would have integrity of content, mission, and motivation. Unfortunately, in my estimation, the leaders of the right-wing takeover lost their roots and become heretical secularists under the sway of a Madison Avenue-type technique and gauge of success. "Whatever works" became misidentified as gospel. The little book *Church Growth That Counts,* was an effort to put into usable form my understanding of the continuing struggle.[9] In that study I used the covenant theme to describe the nature and mission of the people of God, as a theme for evaluating the preparation and process for ministry, and to give insight and perspective to the structure of the

---

[8]See, e.g., Richard Robert Osmer, *A Teachable Spirit* (Louisville: Westminster/John Knox Press, 1990).

[9]Elliott, *Church Growth That Counts* (Valley Forge PA: Judson Press, 1982).

institutional church.

It is rather uncanny that my very last project in theological education as I concluded my work at Colgate Rochester Divinity School was a restructuring of faculty and faculty teams for research, but with primary decisions to be made by the faculty as a committee of the whole in an attempt to facilitate the wholeness of community within the Divinity School as a way of living out the people-of-God model.

Living out the model will continue to be most difficult, as the church in its local and academic expressions seeks to find its way. In the changed social and cultural setting of the post-Constantinian era of the church, we are seeking ways of faithfulness. Even in the South, the homogeneous patterns are disappearing, and I can only regard the struggle for a conservative face for the seminaries as a desperate last-gasp effort to hold on to what was.

The issues to be faced by both the local church and the seminary are, however, universal issues. I can only refer briefly to seven of these issues that in this time will test our faithfulness.[10]

*a. Adult Learners.* In recent years, students have been increasingly in the so-called "adult learner" category. Many of them are second-career people who have come to seminary to pursue a call that earlier was denied *to* them (especially women) or to fulfill an earlier call denied *by* them. Some adult learners seek out a seminary in quest of therapy for a certain woundedness or meaninglessness with which they have been stricken along the way. Also, early retirees are not at all unusual in seminary classes.

One must have great admiration for these people. They and their families often suffer great unsettlement. Their children are uprooted. Often they must cope with a standard of living less than that to which they have been accustomed. They are to be admired for the commitment, sacrifice, and sufferance of required harassments.

Nevertheless, a concern accompanies the admiration. A number

---

[10]I discussed these seven issues elsewhere under the auspcies of the Academic and Theological Education Workgroup of the Baptist World Alliance in a paper prepared for that workgroup at its 1991 annual meeting in Montreal.

of these students arrive at the divinity school with unresolved issues. They often leave with issues still unresolved. Often, especially I suspect on the part of the women, there is anger resulting from being denied encouragement at an earlier stage when a sense of call was experienced. The fragmentation of divorce occurs also, accompanied by a persistent woundedness. One is struck by the number of people in seminary who appear to have been abused in one way or another. It is unlikely these issues will be resolved in the brief time they spend in the theological institution. It is difficult to determine what role the seminary must or can play in providing therapy for such people. "Spiritual formation" is an easy answer, and perhaps a faddish one. Some of the "serendipity" type of spirituality literature, which often suggests a precritical type of thinking, is more of a hindrance than a help in dealing with these and other issues.

Seminary graduates have a plethora of life experiences to contribute to the churches. It is yet too early, however, to determine whether the stresses and the strains they will face in the local church may prove to be a catalyst for evoking their own stresses, or whether the crises they themselves have faced may provide steadying and compassionate guidance for others.

*b. Regionalized Education in a Globalized Setting.* This issue is not new for Southern Baptists, and probably accounts for much of the sheltered provincialism one continues to find.

Increasingly, older students with families find it difficult to travel long distances or to move to distant places in order to get their theological education. Therefore, large numbers are seeking out seminaries closer home. This may serve to handicap the individual in grasping, through broadening experiences, the kind of world in which he or she lives.

Contextualization is an important theme in today's society. The problem with some students is that they are "contextualized" within a very limited setting. Cross-cultural and interdisciplinary experiences become even more important in their theological education. In such cases, issue orientation must increasingly replace abstract conceptualization. Schools must seek diligently to provide planned "immersion" experiences to aid students in their comprehension of the larger world and its peoples. The process necessitates the invitation to our campuses of people from other parts of the globe and of the placement of our students within foreign settings.

Recently, I received a letter from an American Baptist student who is studying in the Baptist Seminary in Managua. When it was indicated that the home seminary in the United States would recognize credits earned at the Managua seminary and that such credits would count toward a degree, the vice rector of the Managua seminary said this was a "first" because traditionally the United States looks despairingly on academic institutions in the third world. Increasingly, cross-cultural and cross-national partnerships must be formed in order to change the climate of training, witness, and mission.

Such education is costly, however, and governing boards are slower than one might wish in realizing that there is a difference between a travel junket and a planned listening experience in life with another people.

*c. Ecumenical Education.* I have always found it painful that Southern Baptists, who have so much to offer, have denied the offering because of their protective isolationism. It is as if what they have to share cannot stand scrutiny.

Student bodies elsewhere are increasingly ecumenical. Some of our schools are intentionally purposive in this direction; others are not quite so sure. Ultimately, all theological education may well be ecumenical education. This raises many issues, such as funding, denominational loyalty, and so forth.

Schools whose student bodies are ecumenically diverse indicate that the church is strengthened in which students discover how much they have in common. Conversely, in an ecumenical setting students are forced to become acquainted with and to come to terms with their own roots, and often this strengthens denominational affiliation.

Yet an ecumenical student body places certain burdens upon the fostering institution. How, for instance, does the school maintain appropriate financial controls and at the same time meet polity and other requirements mandated for five or six denominations? How diverse can a student body be and at the same time maintain the necessary relationship with denominational support groups? At what point does diversity become disuniting?

How should ecumenical diversity affect the makeup of the faculty? Ecumenical education demands an ecumenical faculty. Is there a "critical mass" necessary in order to preserve certain ties?

*d. Academic Achievement and Certification of Promise.* Theological institutions have always struggled with whether their primary responsibility is indoctrination or education, whether the ultimate allegiance is to the church or to the academy, and whether it is possible with integrity to be faithful to both. I have always contended that it *is* possible to be faithful to both. We are most faithful to the church when we are most faithful to the quest for truth.

There is another aspect that has arisen, or at least become intensified in recent years. If we provide an educational context in a theological setting, are we as theological educators responsible to certify the student's readiness for ministry?

One of the results of adult learners and people who enter ministry at a later date is that more and more of them have not had long-term roots in the church. Among such students, lifestyles tend to be more varied and boundaries often are not well set. Those aspects of the Christian gospel traditionally perceived as normative may not hold. In such cases, what is the responsibility of the seminary and what is the responsibility of the local church, judicatory, or denomination?

My "Genesis controversy" critics would have had a ready answer to these questions because they looked upon the seminary primarily as a preacher factory.

For the most part, I suspect that both the churches and the accrediting agency for theological education would like to assume that when students are certified for graduation, they are certified both as to academic achievement and competence for ministry.

There are many disappointments. Some denominations, who have a better defined track for approved entrance into divinity school and into the ordination process, can, at least theoretically, exercise more of an evaluative control. In the free-church system this is not possible. National standards may have been adopted, but practice varies from region to region.

Tensions exist as theological professors complain over the

churches' sometime insistence that the divinity schools "fix" their problems. Some pastors, especially in the right-wing, fundamentalist camp, complain because the school does not succeed in producing "clones" of the sending pastor or of the sending church.

Legal concerns also enter the picture. The courts appear to be sympathetic to those who have met the academic requirements when a school attempts to withhold a degree. Should a seminary allow a student to remain on track for a degree and then deny him or her senior status? Should a school grant a degree but with some possible notation such as "not certified as to promise for ministry"?

It remains to be seen what the outcome of such concerns will be.

*e. Methodology: Theory and Praxis.* This question is closely related to the issue just discussed. In many ways, it underlay the dispute during those early years at Midwestern Seminary.

Seminaries and divinity schools not related to a university have always had to ask how they are like and how they are unlike the university. In what way does a course in New Testament at a seminary differ from a course in New Testament at the university? This is a continuing area of conflict for our professors who wish to be clear about their objective scholarship. Is the professor a sound scholar if he or she weds head and heart? I answered in the affirmative in my Midwestern academic address.

Teaching methodology is also much debated. I was accused of using the "shock" technique at Midwestern Seminary, but the question is much more than an attitudinal one. It is a serious methodological question. When should the method be deductive and when should it be inductive? Is the lecture method appropriate? How does one learn to reflect theologically on matters of issue orientation? How helpful is the case study method?

Younger scholars generally appear to assume that older scholars lean more heavily on the lecture method. Recently I was somewhat amused to hear a younger scholar give a thirty-minute dogmatic lecture on why the lecture method is unacceptable.

A similar debate is generally in evidence between those responsible for the so-called "classical" disciplines and those whose responsibility is for the "practical" disciplines.

Many of today's older seminary students have been, and in

some instances still are, teachers. This fact, no doubt, contributes to the liveliness of the ongoing debate. Scholar-practitioners are increasingly in demand.

*f. Lay Theological Education.* If anything has become certain for me during these past thirty years, the wisdom and necessity of lay theological education is part of that certainty.

During the "Genesis controversy" days, the most perceptive letters received were often those from mothers, homemakers, farmers, teachers, lawyers, day laborers, and an occasional medical doctor.

Certain surveys and conference experiences indicate that our churches are asking our schools for more in quality lay theological education. How does this harmonize with the general mission of the institutions?

Lay people in the churches want quality theological education, the same kind their *professional* church leaders are receiving. They refuse any longer to be held hostage to the pastor's "superior knowledge." Nonordained leadership from time to time expresses the viewpoint that the ordained leadership has failed in its role as teacher and has made improper judgments as to the ability of the church membership to grow in a deeper comprehension of the intellectual as well as the experiential aspects of the Christian faith.

More and more smaller churches are finding it necessary to turn to bivocational or lay pastors. Several denominations indicate that increasingly the clustering of churches with lay leaders, encouraged by a central pastor-mentor, will of necessity be more frequent. United Methodists report that whereas a few years ago sixty active members could support a pastor on minimum salary status, today one hundred members are required to do the same. Where will such lay leaders be trained? Are traditional seminaries and faculties with traditional patterns willing to engage in alternate patterns of education, with night classes, weekends, and other schedules so that weekday workers can attend? Can the ordained and nonordained be trained in the same classrooms at the same time?

*g. Ethnocentric-Multicultural Education.* Our schools and our churches continue to struggle with how best to meet the needs of all segments of society and how to correct serious deficiencies of the past. Are we committed to more than superficial and cosmetic attempts? Even where we are, as for instance in black-church studies and in feminist/womanist studies, can we learn how to balance our so-called Europocentric and male-dominated education without denying the facts of history? Can we learn how to give proper regard and credence to Afrocentric contributions without bringing superficiality to the historical process? Is multicultural education possible without the twin errors of either assimilation or separation into competing groups? In addressing our sins that have erected ghettos, can we avoid those factors that lead to self-ghettoization?

Furthermore, are we willing to pay the price to find and enable the brightest and best of various groups to prepare themselves for leadership? Will we continue to take the course of least resistance and employ whites only because they are the most easily available in a system where others have for so long been denied?

This issue, in particular, calls us to a renewed examination of the very nature of "church."

## Appropriateness of Personal Response

If some or some part of these issues were present even in embryonic fashion in the "Genesis controversy," how well or poorly did I handle or respond to the crisis in which I found myself? The years and experiences since have given me opportunity to consider that question. If there has been continuity between the "Genesis controversy" and the continuing chaos within Southern Baptist life, is there anything by way of response that might have avoided, tempered, or changed the present pattern?

Although my response in those days may have been considered naive, my bottom-line evaluation after all of these years is that (1) there was no other response I could have made that would have been consistent with who I was, and (2) no different response is likely to have changed things very much.

I need to say, however, that the nature of my response has given me a certain amount of concern these many years about two groups of people, namely, (1) seminarians who were wounded or disillusioned and have spent a lifetime as angry people and in some cases as church dropouts, and (2) friends who worked diligently to defend me and who may have felt that I was too detached from their efforts.

I indicated above that for the most part I was really a spectator and not a participant. The political maneuvering was alien to any experience I had known in the church. I really believed that right would win and that right did not have to be defended. To some extent, I still believe that, although I am aware that the reality may not come until the eschaton.

It may be said that my prior experience had not prepared me to know how to engage in such political battle, but I think it was deeper than that. There are times when one must calculate risk and vulnerability and decide to bear a witness with the realization that the witness may prove costly. It was a gift of grace that I could do this without rancor and without any embedded bitterness. It just seemed to be the thing to do. Except for the very small nucleus of power-hungry "plotters" at whom I did become quite angry, I felt that most of the people gathered up in the storm were very sincere and caught up in a system that had trained them to have confidence in their leaders. For most of them, I felt sympathy and even loving concern. That is the way I believe it ought to be within the Body of Christ.

This simple pacifist approach had some dangers about it, however, and I fell prey to those dangers. The fine line between confidence that you are right and following the appropriate path and self-righteousness is thin and brittle. I crossed over that line on several occasions. Perhaps one of the more noticeable times was my prepared statement for the trustees in the September 1962 examination. I compared it with a statement I had presented in December 1961. The 1961 statement had a certain balance and humility to it. The last paragraph of the 1962 statement, however, is embarrassing for its self-righteous arrogance:

> Therefore, the trustees of this institution must decide whether they want on this faculty a man who stands by God's truth as he is given grace to see it, or whether the preference is for one who will perjure

himself in the interests of political imagery.[11]

I am not certain that such a Martin Luther-type statement was necessary, or that it helped. In my opinion, it put me in the same self-righteous pattern with my antagonists.

The other danger to which I refer is the demonic captivity of public attention.

The "trials" and retrials went on for more than a year. There was hardly a day when there was not something on radio or television, or in some magazine, periodical, or newspaper somewhere in the country. I was deluged with church bulletins and quotations from sermons. Even *Time* and *Newsweek* made the matter a focus of their religion pages.[12] I thought I hated all of this and wished it would stop. Then one day it did stop, and I found myself in near depression. Nobody was noticing me anymore. Constant attention for whatever reason can be seriously damaging. After my experience, I can better understand why a beautiful person can go to Hollywood in all innocence, and ultimately become, as many seem to do, a very warped personality. The spotlight can be most demonic. I am grateful that God's grace somehow gave me the ballast needed.

All of this, I think, was the nature of my response. What other response might I have made? I suppose it might have seemed logical to have attempted caucus groups and other kinds of political maneuvering in order to meet the right-wing tactics head-on. Occasionally, I did try plain logic and rational argument. It was soon clear, however, that emotional hysteria does not respond to simple, clear, and logical response. The playing field simply isn't level, and people do not hear each other. The only tactic, then, is to try and politically outwit and outmaneuver. Early on, I discovered this was not to my taste. If you try it, you find yourself giving way to the same emotions, the same anger, and the same ugly tactics as the

---

[11]The written statements for the trustees, December 1961 and September 1962, are in the Seminary records and in my own files.

[12]Cf. "Baptist Split: Southern Baptists," *Time* 80 (9 November 1962) 58; and "Storm over Genesis," *Newsweek* 60 (12 November 1962) 68.

opponents. The bitterness and the ugliness that results does something to human character, and to me that is a worse loss than losing the skirmishes.

In recent years, when the so-called "moderates" in the Southern Baptist Convention declared "holy war" against the right wingers, I felt a sense of caution. As I looked at the newsphotos and into the faces of those who were proclaiming the holy war, people who were theoretically closer to my own theological understandings, I could see them becoming like their fundamentalist opponents in politics, style, and character. This is the most terrible loss of all.

But where does a more passive response leave those who wish to relate to you and who in some sense depend upon you? There were students who were part of my stewardship. Some were so disappointed and hurt by a style and response out of character and out of keeping for the Christian community that they signed off on the Christian ministry and decided to pursue other careers. Was there some other supportive response I might have given that would have prevented such dropouts? Some not only gave up on the ministry, they gave up on the church. That is a burden I have felt all of these years. On the other hand, some students became so angry that they changed denominations. Others stayed with the denomination but have been bitter and even cynics for a lifetime. I have had little concern about the denominational changes, except the pain of losing some of our brightest and best and the empathy when often they have discovered that whatever the polity, some of the same sickness is in every human institution. I have felt great stress for some who have spent their lives with residual bitterness and have felt the necessity of developing a cynical pattern as a way of enduring organizational patterns. I have appreciated the privilege of corresponding with some of these people across the years, but continue to regret the loss of some of the richness of life that an episode so many years ago has cost them. While there can be no organism without some organization, institutional religion must be constantly in a state of rebirth. Yet the maturation, growth, and perfecting of organizational patterns cannot come through cynicism.

There was another sizable group of professors, pastors, students, and other lay leaders who did actively organize and campaign during the "Genesis controversy." I benefited at all times from their concern, and on occasion from their activism. I wish I had documentation available with which to give appropriate recognition to, for example, Robert T. Lathan, Robert E. Winn, Allen G. Woodriff, and Harry L. Reyburn, Jr., who organized Baptists for Freedom. I received great encouragement from the group's support and cannot fathom their ability to spend days and nights and much energy through publications, telephone calls, rallies, and letter writing. I am certain their efforts against authoritarianism helped to inform, enlighten, and encourage many.

Yet, while I benefited from and was often comforted by this group and its activities, I also felt a sense of discomfort. Is it either appropriate or possible to "fight" without using tactics like those distasteful tactics used by the opponents? More than once I shared with my wife the old cliche that we needed to be saved from our friends. Was this, is this just weak smugness on my part? It has certainly often isolated me and denied some collegiality and contact that I have much needed and wanted. I suspect the conclusion for me may be the simple belief that you simply cannot "win" against the right wing in religious brawls. Although the waiting may be long, you wait until right-wingers get into an internal battle as to which of them "really is god," then when they self-destruct you pick up the pieces and get about restoration and healing. It is probably the wounded healer who heals the most and the best.

## Some Learnings about the Pious Ones

Trying to know how to respond to, with, and for the many groups, I did learn much about my own spiritual needs, my personal spiritual nurture, and the reality of spiritual relationship.

I have often thought about the "Genesis controversy" in terms similar to that of my service in the United States Infantry during World War II. In many ways, it was the greatest thing that could have ever happened to me, but may God forbid it should ever happen again! When I was drafted into the army, I thought my world had come to an end. However, it was in the army that I discovered the world, had my horizons broadened beyond Pittsylvania County in Virginia where I was born, and began to grasp something of the varied nature of the human experience. I often wonder how I could ever have served as a pastor had I not learned something about human heartache and the value of listening that my war-service days afforded me. Surely, it was there that I began to grapple with the God who is the God of the cosmos.

Below I will speak of the ecumenical life to which the Genesis experience introduced me; here I need to say only that my life is richer and my world is larger. The valley of trouble does indeed become a door of hope.

All this is probably the case, however, because of the transforming and transformational spiritual realities I was privileged to discover.

Corporate worship at Calvary Baptist Church, Kansas City, provided the redemptive context. Near the beginning of the mess, my wife and I were terribly distraught on a particular Sunday morning as we went for worship on a communion Sunday. It was in the earliest stages of the controversy, and I was about to develop a martyr complex, but that communion worship with those wonderful people made the difference. As I held the communion cup in my hand and looked into the fruit of the vine that reflected the lights of that sanctuary, and sensed the noise of the great silence as we waited in reverence, I suddenly understood the atoning grace of Jesus Christ as never before. There was great strength in that. As the service ended, I found it necessary to stay seated momentarily in order to deal with the almost uncontrollable emotion that seized me with great thanksgiving for God's suffering grace for me. After experiencing the costliness of His sacrifice for me, I don't think I ever felt put upon after that. From that day to this, I have counted the service of communion or Eucharist as the highlight of Christian worship. I am grateful that Word and Sacrament assumed substantive meaning and an essential context for lifelong experience.

Closely akin to corporate worship were the sacred moments with my immediate family around the kitchen table. Initially our little girls were too young to understand, but as we sat around that table and talked together and prayed together, we sensed something together which was beyond understanding. I would not trade those precious times for anything. When we had to leave Midwestern

Seminary and move to a new life at Crozer Theological Seminary and an introduction to American Baptist ways, it was life together around the table that provided the transition for us all. Years later—many years later when our children were adults and long departed from the nest—as Virginia and I prepared to move from Chicago to Colgate Rochester Divinity School, I went ahead and my wife remained behind. She decided to sell much of our old furniture, but we had agreement on one item: we cannot sell the round kitchen table. More than a symbol, it has been an instrument of God's sustaining grace.

A truly strange phenomenon during those days was how the Bible, in an even richer way, became for me a medium of revelation. It had for years been my custom, and still is, to sit quietly at the beginning of the day and read and reflect upon brief segments of Scripture. After a brief time of listening, I generally would write, as I do now, the primary thought on a three-by-five card, stick it in my pocket, and reflect upon it off and on all day. Often it became the germinal seed for private or public prayer, as the occasion demanded. At times, it was a paradox to sit through a committee meeting, a meeting with the right-wing critics, read an article, or listen to some harangue about how I was destroying the Scriptures, and yet at that very moment be able to endure the harangue with some sense of peace and wholeness because I was being nourished by what I had heard through the Scriptures that very day.

I suppose the most significant learning that came, however, was the realization that often those who make the most noise about their piety know the least about its reality. Years later while I was serving as senior pastor of the North Shore Baptist Church in Chicago, the chairperson of our official board occasionally would say to me, "Ralph, when you get these calls from Christian business organizations wanting to be employed by the church for some contract service, be most careful, because the need to promote themselves that way may suggest that they are the least trustworthy." I fully understood his comment.

The attack upon me, upon the book, upon Midwestern Seminary and its president was usually phrased in unctuous verbiage. Letter after letter and article after article would speak of how the particular individual or group had come to its conclusion after a "meeting bathed in prayer." Then I knew that the shotgun blast was coming. People even wrote that they were praying *against* me. In all their anger and intrigue, I don't recall any of the antagonists asking to pray for me, or with me.

Real piety, I discovered, is a deep but quiet stream, and not a noisy, self-advertising cymbal. More than once I learned that the person of deepest piety might be one who had been given the appellation of "liberal" or even "heretic" because he or she violated the machine-stamped mold. A case in point was with Dr. Edwin Dahlberg shortly after I arrived at Crozer Theological Seminary. Dr. Dahlberg himself had been pilloried across the years because of his pacifism, stands for justice, civil rights, and service as president of the National Council of Churches. Heretic and communist were some of the nicer things he was called.

Dr. Dahlberg and I arrived on Crozer campus about the same time. I had come to serve for a year as visiting professor of Old Testament while Dr. Jesse Brown was on sabbatical leave. Dr. Dahlberg had retired as senior pastor of Delmar Avenue Baptist Church in St. Louis and was going to serve for a couple of years as professor of Preaching. I encountered him one day as I was walking through "Old Main" at the seminary. He sensed I was somewhat overwhelmed by all of the changes. He asked if we might talk, and we walked to the tennis courts just outside the building. He asked questions and listened carefully and supportively as I related the stresses and strains of the long months of controversy and now my particular heaviness at being cut off from the Southern Baptist family that gave me birth and for which I continued to have great affection in spite of all the turmoil. I could feel the healing of his pastoral touch. Soon he said, "This needs the context of prayer." Self-consciously, I replied, "Here?" But totally oblivious to the fact that we were on the tennis court, he was already kneeling and beckoned me to join him. Seldom, if ever, have I been carried by such a saint on such beautiful and earnest words to the gates of heaven and ushered into the presence of God. My work at Crozer, and for the remainder of my life, was different after that. I had known conservatives all of my life, but I had never been introduced to that kind of prayer. Here was my encounter with a true liberal, and he introduced me to God. Such a piety has been my continuing quest.

Those months at Crozer Seminary were difficult civil rights days. When Dr. Dahlberg called on me to march with him in front of City Hall or sit with a black family all night in their recently purchased home because the day before whites had gone in and pulled out plumbing and wiring, I was frightened, but I did not hesitate because I knew his integrity and his motivation, and, in particular, the source of his strength.

It was not until later that I learned that Edwin Dahlberg, while a seminary student, had been secretary to Professor Walter Rauschenbusch, the reputed father of the social gospel. Rauschenbusch's social-salvation emphasis sprang from the soil of prayer. Dahlberg was a recipient of that rich legacy, and he shared it with me. I soon discovered the rich resources in many of Rauschenbusch's prayers, a resource I still repeatedly find helpful.[13]

Piety and spirituality are not packaged things, yet I had spent a large part of my Christian life impressed by the packaging. I am so grateful that when the packaging proved to be deceptive, I found the privileged gift on a tennis court.

---

[13]See, e.g., Walter Rauschenbusch, *For God and the People: Prayers of the Social Awakening* (Boston: Pilgrim Press, 1910).

## Chapter 8

# Introduction to the Larger Church

That I have lived my most productive years of ministry outside Southern Baptist life was not of my own initiative. At the time of my dismissal from the seminary, I happened to be involved with two other denominations in some special education projects. There were several opportunities for employment with either of these groups. But the free-church tradition was unusually meaningful to me at that time, and I owed an allegiance to Southern Baptists. A loving witness within appeared to me to be the means of bearing a witness and sharing viewpoints I felt needed to be shared. Although there had been a fair amount of pain, there was no intense bitterness, and I felt equipped to stay within the family and make a positive contribution.

It was not long, however, until I discovered that the kind of mentality that requires a tangible external authority (such as an inerrant scripture) on which to lean, also feels compelled to build walls to protect from any contact with those of another and possibly "contaminating" point of view. Several times, and almost at the point of final contract arrangements with Southern Baptist institutions, pressuring telephone calls to the potential employer led to the conclusion that hiring me was too risky. In one last instance, a pulpit committee unanimously recommended me to a church, and the church voted to extend me a call. Final arrangements about the move were complete, and I went to New York City to attend a professional academic society meeting. I remember what a great sense of peace I felt as I sped across the country from Kansas City to New York.

Hardly had I reached my hotel room, however, when I received a telephone call from the chairman of the committee who suggested that although the church had called me, they had received new information that suggested I ought not to come. It was a number of years later when I discovered there had been a behind-the-scenes strategizing effort to convince the church in question that I was not a "true believer." This did not stop even after I entered another Baptist denomination.

Just prior to my invitation to become the senior minister of the (American Baptist) North Shore Baptist Church in Chicago where I spent thirteen delightful years, a former Southern Baptist official confided to the chairman of North Shore's pulpit committee that there were serious questions about my recognition of the authority of the Scriptures. Fortunately, the chairman of the pulpit committee "read between the lines," and so the effort encouraged rather than discouraged him. (I would add as an aside that I have worked with both the above detractors, one a lay person and the other ordained, in the Baptist World Alliance for many years. It may be difficult for them to read this at this late hour and know that their blocking efforts were shared with me those many years ago.)

This abbreviated recital is unimportant except to say that dogmatists do not give up easily. They feel they have a mission to protect God, and that if they fail to provide such protection, the whole house will fall.

The other significance of this experience is that it is obvious my departure into exile from Southern Baptist life was very reluctant. For many months I waited. It was an active waiting, to be sure, spent primarily in one lecture series after another in colleges and churches. Finally, I did not wish to hear myself lecture on Genesis even once more. So I accepted an offer at Crozer Theological Seminary, proffered some months earlier, and made the transition into the American Baptist community. This was my introduction into a totally different world.

The transition was an important one for me. It was both reluctant and painful, but it gave me a new family. It must be clearly understood that a sense of nostalgia for old roots in no way diminishes a sense of appreciation and thanksgiving for my new family. American Baptists have offered me opportunities I had neither merit nor other right to expect. I must give some impression of this transition so the story I tell can be placed in proper perspective.

## The Biblical Theme of Exile

Exile, journeying, and pilgrimage are some of the most important images in all of biblical history. I have personally discovered that the experiences of exile, journeying, and pilgrimage are the most important exercises in all of life. It is because one is forced to become an exile that one has the privilege of becoming a pilgrim. As a pilgrim, one may be led to make decisions that otherwise would never be made. These are the kinds of decisions that help a person to journey to some of the most important points of one's life. Catapulted by the exile experience, the journeying pilgrim makes discoveries of the soul that otherwise might never have come.

It was said about some of those early faith-believers and Christians that "they acknowledged that they were strangers and pilgrims (that is, exiles) on the earth" (Hebrews 11:13). The writer of 1 Peter approached his early Christian groups with the plea, "I beseech you as strangers and pilgrims . . ." (1 Peter 2:11).

To be a pilgrim is to journey to meaning. It has been suggested that one can travel in a variety of ways. A tourist goes from place to place with no ultimate goals in view except to revert to what was before the travels began. A sojourner may stay for a time in a temporary place with no real interest in either the time, the place, or the people. But, to be a pilgrim is to be on a quest with a particular purpose. Such a person journeys to a foreign country of the soul while being forced to live in a strange and different place, and is thereby forced to make decisions that have to do with the whole value system of life. After such a decision, one is never again what one was before.

I made a wonderful discovery. Forced to live as a pilgrim in exile circumstances, I discovered that the new situation liberated me to clarify who I was and who I ought to be. I would covet for all exiles, that having made the discovery, they can praise God and celebrate the journey, even if the journey into exile was with a push.

## 1. The Necessity of Exile

In all probability, there may be some point in every Christian's life when exile is necessary if one is going to determine for oneself the refinement and ownership of a tradition given by someone else.

An exile is anyone separated from his/her country, or home, or original station, either voluntarily or by stress of circumstance.

It may be physical when you are caused to migrate from one place to another. It may be cultural when you are caused to migrate from one regional or denominational pattern to another. It may be social and economic when you have to find your way in circumstances previously unknown. It may be educational or intellectual. It may be religious when you struggle, both to rescue and redeem traditions from the mossback conservative who has overlaid them with all kinds of hedges and from the flaming and cynical liberal who does not know them.

You are an exile when you recognize you do not fit, when you hear a different drummer for whatever reason, and have to make some determining decisions and grasp some clarifying visions that give a steadying value system to your life. It is a blessing when, given the necessity of exile, we discover and clarify visions that can neither be discovered nor clarified in any other way. Exile may be essential in order that things memorized by rote actually become your own, in new form and shape, through the exilic experience.

## 2. The Example of Biblical Patterns

Exile was the most important time in the life of Israel. The greatest theological insights came in those days when Israel had no temple, and, languishing in a strange land where they were taunted and tormented, they went through the night of the soul to discover that religion is not a place but rather a relationship, a relationship that provides a grace greater than any place. The psalmist could continue to cry, "If I forget you, O Jerusalem, let my right hand wither!" But the cry for Jerusalem was more than a nostalgic cry for a place. Jerusalem was far more than a place. It was a code word for God, for a tradition of faith, for God's dealings with a people, and a symbol of hope for the future. It took an exile to break the staleness of a Jerusalem that was primarily a place and to bring the sudden realization that there is no worthwhile today and surely no vibrant future until one experiences a faith relationship with the very God from whom life had sprung.

Job, an exilic (not a patriarchal) character found in a postexilic book, was learned in religion, but it was not until he was caught in the nightmarish exile of his life that he could say, "I had heard of thee with the hearing of my ear, but now I see thee with the seeing of my eye" (Job 42:5).

It is worth any exile to come to the place where you can see in a way you never saw before.

The blessings of the exilic life were perhaps first tasted by Abraham, who "went out." Those blessings were more seriously focused and formalized in Moses. Severed from the faith roots of Abraham, Isaac, and Jacob, Moses floated for a while in the Egyptian system. But one day when he saw his own kind being beaten into slavery, he became anxious to know who he was. In that anxiety, he fled to the backside of the mountain to come to grips with himself, and with God.

Exile prepares us to contribute even when others cannot see the possibilities. So Moses went back to lead his people out, and "Pharaoh did not know that they were gone" (Exodus 14:5). When the tribal peoples found themselves in an exodus from Egypt, they were in an exile of sorts. Moses could help them see some things they could not at first see. He saw manna on the ground. Not everyone may see manna on the ground, but thank God for the pilgrimage experience of the exile that enables one to see.

There were many other exiles in Israel's life. For forty years, they roamed around in a wilderness, lost and without direction. Joshua (Joshua 24) has the responsibility of detecting whether they had learned anything, experienced anything, or decided anything during the forty years of wilderness exile.

Even the biblical leaders recognized there was nothing magic about an exile. Joshua's crowd was a mixed mob. For some, the rugged years had led to a virility of faith and a spiritual toughness. But for others, it had meant only an unsettledness. They carried with them the pagan ornaments of the Egyptians and the Canaanites.

There was doublemindedness, restlessness, and indecision. Exile had meant only a capitulation to contemporary thought forms, doubts, and pagan practices. How one responds determines whether one becomes a "pilgrim" in an enforced exile.

Standing in sharp contrast to indecision was Joshua, for whom the wilderness exile had only polished the diamond of personal faith. His life-pattern had been set at an earlier time when, along with Caleb, he had been sent to look over the Promised Land. Only he and Caleb maintained confidence in the divine promise. It was part of who he was to call out as the test of a confederacy of faith: "Choose for this day whom you will serve, whether you will serve the Lord, or the gods of the Amorites . . ." (Joshua 24:15).

That's what an exile and a wilderness experience force you to do. It forces one to make decisions and to clarify what those decisions mean. It necessitates that one struggle with something and with someone, and ultimately, to clarify what is real, and what is not, even about one's religion.

### 3. The Personal Response to Exile

It may appear self-serving, and can easily become arrogant and egocentric, but I want now to make a transition to the existential exile of my departure from Southern Baptist life. But, I would have you remember that a pilgrim is not one who has arrived, but one who is traveling on to a destination not yet reached.

I spent my early years with a loving group of people, singing often about the old-time religion:

> Gimme that old-time religion,
> Gimme that old-time religion, . . .
> It was good for my father (etc.),
> And it's good enough for me. . . .

But one day—in a sense not until I was 38 years old—I discovered by being exiled from all that was near and dear to me at that time, that you cannot have your father's religion. There must come a time, through the night of the soul, when you know it is yours, and neither your father nor your mother could ever really give it to you.

I was a so-called hothouse variety Christian. Signing on was no difficult task, for everything about my culture, my family, and my setting was geared in a religious direction. It would have been more difficult to say "no" to a religious commitment than it was to say "yes." Even in high school (in violation of church-state tradition), I was much of the time president of the student government and operated in a pattern that allowed me to start every student council meeting with prayer and sermonettes. Artificially and oppressively, as I look back upon it, I was seeking to mold people into my own dogmatically conservative mold, and thoughtlessly forcing the two Jewish members of our group to surrender their freedoms and perhaps to suffer hurt.

My first glimpse of exile, forcing me to get beneath the surface of what had been handed to me on a cultural platter, was a period of service in the army, primarily on duty in the winter's cold of Europe where for the first time I saw people die, watched people go to hell and back, and began to recognize that some of the easy shibboleths handed to me were surface deep and did not hold.

I made progress during that phase of exile, a progress in spiritual depth and in the recognition of the superficiality of some things that had been handed to me. But it was much like Israel's wilderness years, for much was yet unclear, and when life became easy again the clarifying struggle was not so necessary.

Suddenly, years later, I found myself as a young professor, advantaged beyond many in my biblical field, easily handing out answers to age-old questions. One day my answers did not fit. I was humbled from my inadvertent arrogance, cut off from my professorship, cut off from my beloved Southland, cut off from those I had thought were my friends, and living in exile. I have lived the remainder of my life in religious and physical exile, no longer fitting into the right-wing culture I once embraced and never fitting into the cynicism of a liberal theological culture where a surface humanism is often accompanied by cynicism.

Initially I wandered, until in the dark night I discovered that at a depth far beneath the theological dogmas and forms I knew so well was a God of experience, often hidden by the very religion I was seeking to defend. That was when I began to discover, beyond any religious or denominational labels, others who shared the same experience of grace. It was an enforced journey within the rich exile of the soul that helped me discover that there is a spiritual newness that makes the defense of old fences unnecessary and undesirable—that God carries me and that I do not have to carry God.

The conclusion of my experience is: worry not about exile, for exile is not bad. Exile is when you begin to grow and claim the divine-human experience as your very own. It is when you are forced to probe beneath the tidy doctrinal catechism whose words you may have memorized as a child. In exile, you really do have to choose which God or gods you are going to serve. It may be the same God your fathers served in the old place, but the exile forces circumstances upon you that in turn force decisions between what is God and what is idolatry, what is religion and what is relationship. In the exile, you discover that the fruits of the Spirit are not something you decide to have and reach for through some legalistic action. They are things that happen because you are living in the house of love that has come about, not because you signed on to dogma or to a denomination's program, but because in the depths of your being, you have heard the "invitation to intimacy" and have accepted Christ's invitation: "Make your home in me, as I make mine in you" (John 15:4).

It is because of the exile experience that I discovered a value system that would hold, one which had been there all along, but which at times was squelched by the external form in which it was conveyed. Exile may enable one to dig beneath the conformist creeds and find the bedrock attitudes and relationships that govern all of life and give response to crises, providing anchor in the storm and compass for the journey. Even yet I miss some of the sights and sounds of the old home, but I am grateful for the growth beyond.

When Elie Wiesel was awarded the Nobel Peace Prize, the *Christian Century* said of him:

> His own life is the story of enforced citizenship in the kingdom of night—his name for Auschuitz—and a long, long journey, stretching over decades, before any glimmer of true dawn entered that darkness

and gave faint signs of a possible sunrise.[1]

Wiesel had traveled through a long and lonely exile, but always pushing the darkness back, until, having traveled through the exile, he could say in its acceptance:

> No one is more capable of gratitude than one who has emerged from death's kingdom. Every moment is a gift of grace . . . Our lives are no longer our own.[2]

Of course, there is no comparison between the Holocaust experience and my "mini exile." Nevertheless, I find the words so appropriate because exile has been a gift of grace within new realms of light which otherwise might have remained hidden for a lifetime.

## Discoveries in the Larger Church

It is somewhat intentional that the above themes of exile have been self-serving. It has been necessary for me to bear this testimony in order that I might share some of the exilic discoveries whose realization and growth might have remained closed to me had I remained within the fold of my birthing denomination.

### 1. The Larger Church (Ecumenicity)

Perhaps the greatest blessing of the exile was the existential introduction to the larger church in its ecumenical dimensions. Before 1962-1963, I had worked with other denominations, frequently made "forays" into the territory of other denominational groups to give lectures and workshops, and was active in the founding of a cross-denominational theological society. Although I did not recognize it at the time, however, I now realize I was not truly ecumenical in my understanding of the oneness of the church. The work I did was no doubt unconsciously motivated by my rootage in Southern Baptist life in the sense of having something to "take to others" who were of a somewhat benighted nature. I had not really

---

[1]Robert M. Brown, "Elie Wiesel: Writer as Peacemaker," *The Christian Century* 103 (5 November 1986) 964-65.
[2]Ibid.

"lived" in the larger church or ever seriously contemplated the ecumenical nature of the church. I now appreciate ecumenicity as the very essence of the church; in those days, I was neither prepared to remove my narrow denominational spectacles nor to listen to the biblical tradition on that score. It was endemic in my context to go to the Scriptures in search of a particular design and support. I suspect I had never given serious thought as to the "catholic" nature of the church, in either its Protestant or Roman Catholic dimensions.

*a. The Protestant Dimension.* Although supposedly a "liberal" to many Southern Baptists, in those early days I was still constrained by the rather landmarkist view that said Baptists were not part of the "Protestant" community. Baptists are unique. I am not sure I ever tried to trace Baptists from the early Christians, but I was greatly influenced by the Graves and Pendleton emphasis that it was possible to pursue a "restoration" of the practices of the early church.[3] This view, of course, did not acknowledge any great debt to the Reformation. This admission makes it clear that my basic theological understanding of the church at the time was ill-formed, although perhaps in the process of formation, but composed of many ambiguous elements, often joined together in illogical fashion and with much inconsistency. My views of Scripture were increasingly liberated, but I suspect that happened because the professional nature of my position as a professor of Old Testament forced me to consider many viewpoints and a great variety of evidence from many quarters. Up until the time of the conflict, there had been no circumstances that forced me to do this with regard to my understanding of the church. The entire milieu of my life up to that point had been that of championing, and at times defending, the "church" of which I was a part. This readily points out the danger when any individual Christian or group of Christians exist in isolation.

Shock therapy was perhaps necessary for me, as it may be for many. My first day on the campus of Crozer Theological Seminary in Chester, Pennsylvania helped with the therapy. Some kind of

---

[3]Cf. Robert F. Torbet, *A History of the Baptists* (Valley Forge PA: Judson Press, 1963) 281-82.

meeting of older alumni was taking place, and one of those present from the 1920s era walked up to me and said, "Welcome, Elliott; I am an old unreconstructed liberal myself, and we are glad to have you." He misunderstood who I was and what motivated me, but it was one of the factors that forced me to think through my relationship with the larger church that had transpired during those few years at Midwestern, and ultimately to come to the recognition that Baptists of any description are but a small part of the church and with very human and imperfect understandings at that. It was actually a great relief to be able to give up the deception that there was some kind of monolithic ecclesial pattern in the New Testament and to join in an appreciation of the varied ecclesial patterns with their positive contributions from various times and settings of the church.

As our shrinking world forces people from their homogeneous confines into heterogeneous settings of all kinds—whether cultural, racial, or otherwise—I suspect many of the Baptists who have been led to believe they "have it" in ways other groups do not are going to share many of the resentments I increasingly experienced with my growing awareness of the ecumenical nature of the church. My life has been singularly blessed in the belated discovery that ecumenical oneness is the given nature of the church. I am pleased with the circumstances that delivered me from an isolationist and isolating Christianity into the richness of cooperative Christianity. It was a joy to discover, contrary to what I had been led to believe, that early Baptists were far more inclusive. In their rather "catholic" confessional statements, they often began with those things held in common with other denominations before going on to delineate those aspects that were the particulars of Baptist understanding. Under the leadership of John Smyth, that early 1612 Baptist group suggested that "all penitent and faithful Christians are brethren in the communion of the outward church, wheresoever they live, by what name soever they are known." General Baptists in 1678 stressed their desire to "unite and confirm all true Protestants."[4]

---

[4]Ralph H. Elliott, ed., "American Baptists: A Unifying Vision," *American Baptist Quarterly* 6/2 (June 1987) 84-90.

It is of great comfort to me to know that our heritage is not characterized by an exclusivistic attitude and that what some have presented as "Baptist belief" is a distortion of our roots.

The freedom to examine the contributions from all denominations helped me to discover and appreciate the nature of covenant as being part of the significant center of religious life. This deepened my understanding of baptism and church in particular.

The forced necessity of examining who I was and whence I had come also prepared me for three tasks in life which brought me particular joy. Two of them were within the Protestant sector. I speak particularly of my service with American Baptists as chairperson of the Commission on Denominational Identity. The materials produced by that effort continue to form the primary basis of the denomination's attempt to reclaim and to renew its heritage.

The other matter that came at the end of my professional career was that of service as vice president for academic life and dean of faculty for an ecumenical divinity school.[5]

*b. The Roman Catholic Dimension.* The mention above of "three tasks in life" enables me to make transition to a privileged part of my journey, an experiential and intellectual appreciation of the Roman Catholic part of the Christian family.

During my childhood I knew no Roman Catholics and had heard of the church only through the many presentations of its evil designs and its anti-Christ character of subverting the world. In my home community, there was a one-room Catholic structure, but there appeared to be little activity. The local bakery imported a baker and his family named "Brosky," and this Roman Catholic family moved in next door to us. In all our relationships, however, religion was never mentioned, so we thought of them as "people," not "Catholics." You simply could not be Catholic without being evil, and the Brosky's were not evil, so we disassociated them from their church.

---

[5]Colgate Rochester Divinity School/Bexley Hall/Crozer Theological Seminary in Rochester, New York. Although American Baptists and Episcopalians are the primary constituent bodies, students come from all denominations. The school is in a covenant relationship with St. Bernard's Roman Catholic Seminary which provides Catholic students as part of the mix.

That aura hauntingly carried over into my adult life and changed very little during my early teaching years. I did not attack Catholics because such a negative posture would not harmonize with my understanding of the positive and affirming nature of the Christian gospel. I was more comfortable ignoring the Catholic world, although there was still the "evil empire" suspicion within me.

In contrast to those days, since 1971 I have worn every day of my life a watch presented to me by the Roman Catholic Diocese of Albany, New York, a watch warmly inscribed on the back. For longer than that, a paperweight, always on my desk, is the signet medallion handed to me when I participated in the service of installation for the incoming diocesan presiding bishop. These two items, the watch and the medallion, are symbols of the enrichment of my life upon "coming into another world of the church." I am certain this would never have happened without the exile.

After a transitional stint on the faculty of Crozer Theological Seminary in Chester, Pennsylvania, I moved to Albany, New York to become senior pastor of Emmanuel Baptist Church, American Baptist. I had never before lived as a religious minority, a renegade Baptist in a community that was eighty-six percent Roman Catholic. It was a difficult beginning because there were two mixed-marriage funerals for which I had to officiate during the first few weeks, and in both instances I was denied participation in the Catholic cemetery. My emotions were about to tell me that the evil things I had heard about the Roman Church were true. Through an interesting set of circumstances, however, I was thrown into contact with a number of priests and other "religious" within the diocese who were struggling with a pilgrimage almost identical to my own: how to move from sterile dogmatism to relational Christianity. (That term "religious," by the way, is here a noun, singular or plural, that refers to a member or members of a religious order, under monastic vows.) The nomenclature was different and the system was different, but the struggle was basically the same. I found myself attending serious Bible study groups in the diocese, participating in discussions related to the ferment of Vatican II, and then regularly teaching each semester in the local Franciscan college, Siena College, and in Our Lady of Angels Seminary. Some of the most serious Bible study and truly "evangelical" spirit I ever experienced was with the people in the diocese.

I tried to share something of the similarities of the struggle in a little essay "Strange Bedfellows," in the book *Should Preachers Play God*.[6] My basic thesis, which for me still holds, is that in the United States, "pre-Vatican II Roman Catholics and Protestant Christians whose churches have reflected the patterns of their cultural and sociological surroundings (especially the Southern church) are almost identical in their approach to the question of authority."[7] Especially after these years of observing the antics within the ongoing Southern Baptist struggle, I want to affirm what I wrote:

> Roman Catholics of the post-Vatican II lifestyle are making more progress on the question than are orthodox Christians whose polity gives lip service to freedom but who have not discovered that sometimes unstructured democracy can be the worst tyranny—a horrible tyranny when "charismatic" individuals capture it. Often people who despise *tradition* have a strong unwritten tradition which not only becomes a test of faith, but which is subject to all kinds of "authoritative" manipulation.[8]

Forced to study the documents of Vatican II and invited to participate in the life and worship of the Roman Church, I was able to borrow the rich tradition of liturgy to enrich my shallow worship. "Sacrament," rightly understood, became a meaningful word for me whereby my own negative and "light" tradition of ordinances has been enriched beyond measure. Years of contact with my Roman Catholic seminary students and participation in the journeys of my Roman Catholic colleagues for many years now have made me far more appreciative of the richness to be found in the true "catholicity" of the church. These relationships have introduced me to the "base" communities of Central and South America and have helped me to become a world Christian in the quest for liberation and freedom.

---

[6]Claude A. Frazier, comp., *Should Preachers Play God* (Independence MO: Independence Press, 1973) 206-24.
[7]Ibid.
[8]Ibid.

Before I moved from the Roman Catholic Diocese of Albany, New York, I was employed by the diocese to participate with Reginald Fuller, an Episcopal New Testament scholar, and Daniel Maguire, a Roman Catholic ethicist, in the development of a program of continuing education for the priests and religious of the diocese. It has been a privilege to watch the growth of that program and to return to New York state in more recent years and, through my association with St. Bernard's Roman Catholic Seminary in its affiliation with Colgate Rochester Divinity School, to go to Albany again and help with the present pattern of that continuing education program which was begun so many years ago.

My conclusion after a lifetime of association with the Roman Catholic Church, aware of its history and many aberrations, is that institutional religion is constantly diseased and must be subjected to a continuous state of scrutiny and rebirth. I affirm my identity as a reformed and reforming Protestant. Nevertheless, my growth in relational and ecumenical Christianity has been aided far more by the Catholic part of the family than by the Protestant side. In these shallow days, as a bankrupt Protestant church seeks to recapture its essence and appropriate form in local churches, my hope is that the Catholic church may become enthusiastic in a renewed way once again in its ecumenical patterns. It has been my observation, especially in urban communities, that the richness of cooperative Christianity in its revitalizing spirit is fluent only when the local diocese of the Roman Catholic Church strongly commits itself to the ecumenical and reforming spirit.

## 2. The Larger Church (Spirituality and the Scriptures)

This brings me almost full circle to where I began. My interest in the Scriptures, an interest that got me into trouble, was never as an end in itself. It was part of my personal hunger for growth in a mature kind of spirituality. Something within me has always said that a wholistic spiritual life was multidimensional and could not be compartmentalized. My Old Testament study (see Isaiah 6) had early brought me to a realization of the necessity of reaching out to God, reaching out to self, and reaching out to the world. Although this certainly had not achieved the sacramental view of life that I came to appreciate later, I did sense that the biblical message has to be the context for such a spirituality. I must confess that already by the time of *The Message of Genesis* I was aware of the shortcomings of a person-centered, singularly person-in-isolation orientation for spirituality, and was struggling with the corporate and ecclesial nature of spirituality. That, however, provided the stifling framework—an approach to Scripture that was literalistic, sterile, and dogmatic, and an attachment to church that was inflowing rather than outgoing.

The cosmic nature of spirituality had not yet dawned upon me, yet glimpses and intimations had come through my Genesis studies and through the creation psalms. Insights from New Testament books such as Ephesians and Colossians were not yet fully realized. Spirituality in my early years was measured by what we did *not* do. We survived by what we were *against*. The concept of spirituality would have been somewhat meaningless to us had we not been able to find something or someone to attack. This was clearly unsatisfactory, so I struggled with the two above foci as the possible route to deeper and more experiential understanding, that is, the nature of the biblical revelation and the nature of the church.

A propositional approach to Scripture did absolutely nothing for my internal nurture, and an isolated and isolating church built around a superficial serendipity left me empty and with no motivation for being. Although I still am not satisfied with my growth in these areas, I thank God for the necessity of the exilic journey, else I apparently would have continued to be stuck in the same externalities of those early days and still caught in the irrelevances of a "successful" church.

*a. The Scriptures.* Higher criticism was my tool for probing the nature of the Scriptures, but I recognized some serious deficiencies in that approach. I sought to deal with those deficiencies in "Direction in Old Testament Studies," my inaugural Midwestern Seminary academic address.

The use of higher criticism was of tremendous help to me in spite of its deficiencies. I regret that some who know better have played into the hands of the literalists and fundmentalists with their

suggestion that "historical biblical criticism is bankrupt."[9] Popular-
izers of the spirituality fad have picked up such blanket statements
and have attributed to higher criticism the responsibility for the lack
of experiential religion. Ben Johnson lumps it into a category, and
says:

> The historical-critical approach to Scripture, liberal theology of the
> early part of this century, neoorthodoxy at its midpoint, and liberation
> theology at its close—all have lacked effectiveness in deepening the
> minister's personal experience of God.[10]

I don't believe any of the above claimed to be the antidote for one's
lack of spirituality. What I do know is that a historical-critical
approach to Scripture, with all its limitations, helped release me
from a sterile and wooden orthodoxy, which gave me a "correct"
belief but which was a wall against, not a tool for, experiential
religion.

There is more to value than condemn in higher criticism.
Without it, one would be hard-pressed to work one's way through
the cultural, social, economic, and political factors and free the text
to become a vehicle for revelational expression and experience.
Critical tools alone are insufficient, but it is unwise to make such
statements as encourage people to return to precritical understandings of Scripture. I fully agree with Edgar McKnight that "a
satisfying approach cannot be uncritical, but it must move beyond
the critical."[11] Biblical criticism is not an attempt at explanation.
Rather biblical criticism offers some tools with which to "get at" the
explanation. Rather than throwing the tools away, we must go
beyond. All of the tools in the world will not build a house unless
you use the tools with a certain purpose in view.

David Gracie points out the travesty of a "biblical fundamental-
ism" which "poisoned the well with . . . literal, narrow, and

---

[9]E.g., Walter Wink, *The Bible in Human Transformation: Toward a New Paradigm
for Biblical Study* (Philadelphia: Fortress Press, 1973) 1.

[10]Ben Campbell Johnson, *Pastoral Spirituality* (Philadelphia: Westminster Press,
1988) 109.

[11]Egard V. McKnight, *Postmodern Use of the Bible* (Nashville: Abingdon Press,
1988) 14.

unloving interpretations of Scripture."[12] Gracie affirms the validity of an alternative higher criticism that brings us an "objectifying" of Scripture, but then points to a "subjective" experience of the Word for which the objectifying step is but a vehicle.[13] The objectifying and the subjective experiences are the two steps in Dietrich Bonhoeffer's process of meditation.

The objectifying of Scripture allows the best use of biblical criticism in studying a Bible book in order to determine the best text, the nature of the literature, and the contextual understanding of the who, when, why, where, and for what purpose the passage was produced. However, step 1, the objectifying, feeds into step 2, the "subjective experience," the "listening" to what the objectifying tool has uncovered. Intellectual understanding is insufficient, for, as Bonhoeffer suggested, "I do not treasure God's promise in my understanding but in my heart."[14] We must find a way to let the Word penetrate deeply and dwell within us like "the Holy of Holies in the sanctuary."[15] The coalescence of the objectifying and the subjective allows us to discover both the social and political setting that necessitated and produced the Word in the first place and likewise the way we receive the Word and experience our own social and political reality.[16]

Reflection on the Midwestern experience forced me to move far beyond where I was so as to better perceive how the Holy Spirit could bless the words and use them to convey the relevant Word in current circumstances. I was thus prepared in later years to be sympathetic to and empathetic with Christians in third world countries as they have listened under the banner of what some have called "liberation theology" to the relevant and liberating Word in an oppressive society.

Although the so-called "hermeneutics of suspicion" does not

---

[12]In Dietrich Bonhoeffer, *Meditating on the Word,* ed. and trans. David McI. Gracie (New York: Ballantine Books, 1986) 1.
   [13]Ibid., 2.
   [14]Ibid., 8.
   [15]Ibid.
   [16]Ibid., 7.

appeal to me,[17] I readily admit that "truth is neither wholly in the past nor solely within the world of the interpreter."[18] I recognize that the Word is a product of the interaction of the two, and I am forced to be "suspicious of the interests brought to the exegetical task"[19] by me or by anyone else. In an earlier day, I assumed one might accumulate a certain biblical knowledge and then seek to apply it. Now I know, or at least strongly believe, a belief borne by experience, that revelation must be mediated. This brings me great excitement as I sense not only that God through the Spirit has worked in the inspiration and preservation of the Scriptures, but that the Spirit is no less active today in quickening the Scripture to create a new Word.

Had the word "deconstruct" been coined thirty years ago, some of my critics would have welcomed its availability to describe what they thought I was doing to the Scripture—"tearing it apart." I am pleased, however, to have had the enforced reflection of the years of exilic experience which have led me to find meaning in Leonardo Boff's suggestion that in Scripture interpretation,

> To deconstruct means to see the building in terms of the construction plan and redo the construction process, pointing up temporal nature and possible obsolescence of the representational materials, while at the same time, revealing the permanent value of its import and intent.[20]

In spite of what some of my critics thought, my approach to the Scriptures in those days was very conservative. Although we certainly occupied different rooms, some of my critics and I lived in the same house. My major concern then was with the stability of the Scripture, as it was. The years have taught me that the Scripture is much larger than that, that there is something mysterious about its nature and that its revelational prowess increases and grows. This

---

[17]See the work of Elisabeth Schussler Fiorenza, *In Memory of Her* (New York: Crossroad Publishing Co., 1989) 56, along with that of certain other feminist theologians.

[18]David Batstone, *From Conquest to Struggle* (Albany: State University of New York Press, 1991) 150.

[19]Ibid., 149.

[20]Ibid., 134n.112.

gives me an even greater sense of awe and a deeper appreciation of the transcendent. Perhaps it has been the mixed combination of experience, process thought, and metaphysical philosophy, but I now feel strongly that variation and differentiation keep the Scripture from ever being "a one-time thing," tied to one particular age. There is something inherent in the principle of Scripture that drives it on to something else and enables it to retain its timelessness. A dynamic view is far more helpful to me than a static one, and so I have come to understand there is more in the moving and changing than there is in the immutable.[21] Another way to say it is that the immutable is known only through that which moves and changes.

It has been thrilling to be engaged in this divine-human fabric. The result is an appreciation of the divine-human nature of both church and Scripture as set in the context of an understanding of the divine-human Jesus who is neither God, nor usurps the place of God, but is ever faithful as the bridge providing a relationship with God.

*b. The Church.* In speaking of the church as a growth experience in my exilic life, I refer particularly to the church in its corporate covenantal and cosmic dimensions. My early study of the Old Testament had introduced me to the concept of corporate personality whereby the individual with personal experiences and personal responsibilities and functions might find his or her true identity only in a unity of the whole. At the same time, the unity of the whole might find its expression through the individual. There is no "I" without the community and no community without the "I." Although I think he nowhere attributes his understanding to the Old Testament, Dietrich Bonhoeffer devotionally expressed the corporate personality perspective when he wrote, "Let him who cannot be alone beware of community. . . . Let him who is not in community beware of being alone."[22] Nevertheless, the emphasis among

---

[21]Cf. Henri Bergson, *An Introduction to Metaphysics,* trans. T. E. Hulme (New York: Macmillan Publishing Co., 1955) 54.

[22]Bonhoeffer, *Life Together,* trans. John W. Doberstein (New York: Harper & Row, 1954) 77.

Southern Baptists had been so individualistic that it was many years before I could move from the individual to the corporate to the cosmic understanding with the realization that I am related not only to a corporate body called "church," but to everything in all of creation through a relationship with the God of the cosmos.

The Old Testament (and of course the New Testament) makes it so clear that God is the God of the cosmos that it is difficult to comprehend how one could work within that context and at the same time be blinded by such an individualistic view of salvation and everything else. Such a limited view demonstrates the strong emotional binding of the distorted and restrictive local church setting. It was not until my exilic years that an enlarged ecumenical, corporate, and cosmic perspective helped me better understand some of the liberating emotions that had transpired along the way, and to have a sense of peace about beliefs and actions that differed from my heritage. Let me use a communion experience from my basic training days in the army as an illustration.

During the first weeks of "basic training," trainees cannot leave camp, so on Sundays I could not go off post to find "my kind" of church. My legalistic religious background mandated that I attend a worship service on Sunday, or my guilt simply would not go away. Although worship with people of other backgrounds and denominations at the army chapel was a new experience, I found it to be meaningful and most satisfying. This was true, that is, until communion time. I had heard all of my life that Baptists could not commune with others without violating one's own beliefs and placing approval on all kinds of "heresies." So during communion at the chapel I would abstain, and feel simply miserable during that part of the service.

One day it occurred to me that these soldiers had voluntarily chosen, in spite of many obstacles, to make worship a part of their experience at that basic training center. So later, when the communion elements were passed, I found myself reaching for them. When I did so, it was as if I literally heard chains drop from my wrist to the floor of the post chapel, and I looked down to see those chains there. There was a sense of liberation, freedom, and kinship that I could not explain. Much of the "Genesis controversy" had to do with putting me back in those shackles.

Paul D. Hanson had not yet written what I consider to be one of the most helpful expositions of ecumenical understanding, *The People Called. The Growth of Community in the Bible*, in which he posed T. S. Eliot's question, "What life have you if you have not life together?"[23] My studies in Genesis had begun to give me materials for such clarification, but the intellectual and the emotional pilgrimage did not come together until later. In *The Message of Genesis*, I spoke of "the sociological implications of sin."[24] The unity with all of humankind is obvious in Genesis 10 and 12. The people-of-God emphasis, which the 1 Peter 2:9-10 borrowed from Exodus 19:5-6, denied any further existence as an isolated individual.

It was my friendship with Jitsuo Morikawa, American Baptist director of evangelism, associate general secretary of American Baptist Churches, and world Christian, that enabled me finally to find solace as a child of the universe.[25] I was very fortunate to have Jitsuo Morikawa as an early mentor in American Baptist life and owe much of my present understanding to his help. More than any other one individual, he helped me realize that there can be no "mono" spirituality in the sense of something invested in my being and my being alone. He helped me understand my own spirituality in terms of a wholistic identity with creation and to accept my humanness as an extension of the created world.

My Old Testament background, when freed from imported Greek Gnostic tendencies, prepared me to appreciate the cosmic Christ, the cosmic order, and the cosmic world. I was helped tremendously by Morikawa's effort at a "regenerative theological vision"[26] which sought to "respiritualize" the natural order, centered on the cosmic Christ who is "the image of the invisible God" and who "is before all things" and in whom "all things hold

---

[23](San Francisco: Harper & Row Publishers, 1986) 1.

[24]*The Message of Genesis* (Nashville: Broadman Press, 1961) 52-53.

[25]See my "Spirituality as Power for Renewal," in the forthcoming *Prophet for the Twenty-first Century: Jitsuo Morikawa*, ed. Owen D. Owens (1992).

[26]I borrow the phrase from Gary Dorrien, *Reconstructing the Common Good* (Maryknoll NY: Orbis Books, 1989).

together" (Colossians 1:15-17). My appreciation for other world religions and the relationship of other world religious communities to the Christian community evolved from my dialogue with Jitsuo Morikawa over a period of many years. How these religious communities relate to the environment and a "sustainable future" became an interest for me for which Jitsuo laid the groundwork.[27] I am tremendously grateful for the many events and persons, and to Dr. Morikawa in particular, who helped me to find a new way of looking at the church and at the world, and for making me want to discern the activity of God in the midst of the world and thus to proclaim Him as Lord of all.[28]

• • •

Many today struggle to characterize our time and to understand the place of the church in such a time. Descriptions include such terms as premodern, modern, and postmodern. We hardly need help in understanding the premodern age. Those in control among Southern Baptists thirty years ago, and certainly those in control today, would have us leave the modern age and its mechanistic approach to life and return to or preserve the premodern period.

It is an encouraging sign that people in almost every field of endeavor, including specialized sciences, and physics especially, while appreciating the rich contributions of the Enlightenment and the age of science, are now recognizing the inadequacy of the modern period's mechanistic approach to life and are calling for a *post*modern recognition that some sense of the transcendent is absolutely essential if the human is to survive.

So I am very grateful that circumstances forced me out of the kind of closed community of church which is inadequate for post-modernism. I must confess I do not know the shape of Christ's

---

[27]See, e.g., Herman E. Daly and John B. Cobb, Jr., *For the Common Good* (Boston: Beacon Press, 1989).

[28]For those who have not had the privilege of Dr. Morikawa's discerning insights, I suggest the reading of the brief biography *Footprints*, written by his wife Hazel Takii Morikawa and published by Jennings Associates in 1990.

community in the world of the future, but my forced pilgrimage has helped me to become a "world affirmer" and to support the view that this is God's world, that there is an underlying goodness in creation and in human personhood, and that despite the agony about us, "the earth . . . is not just a veil of tears but a womb filled with life."[29]

[29]Harvey Cox, *The Silencing of Leonardo Boff* (Oak Park IL: Meyer Stone Books, 1988) 34.

# Conclusion

All the way through the thoughts expressed in this manuscript, my mind keeps bumping into a phrase that expresses a conclusion I have reached, yet one I do not like. The phrase is "Eulogy for a Great Tradition." There is still talk of freedom and religious liberty, but it has been a long time since these were allowed to be actualized in practice in Southern Baptist life. Compromisers seeking for some personal-security life raft contributed to the death of religious liberty. Such compromise is sin, and it contributes to the harlotry of a huge religious body in this country that can no longer proclaim itself as the "people of God." Arrogant self-righteousness claims the preservation of orthodoxy, but the agonizingly candid messages and symbols of the prophet Hosea are probably more accurately descriptive.

The chaos for which the "Genesis controversy" was but a mild prelude continues. Doublespeak persists. In more recent months, news releases have heralded a "Covenant of Renewal" at Southern Baptist Theological Seminary in Louisville. When I read that future faculty openings will be filled with "conservative evangelical scholars," however, I see this grasp for a lifeboat as simply more nails in the coffin, a shroud for a great tradition.

I read in personal letters from seminary faculty and even in the press[1] that people who are hurting are trying to save their jobs or work with both sides until something else or something better comes along. Not able to depend on either "the arrogance and militancy of

---

[1]See, e.g., "Losing and Learning in Denominational Conflict," a "personal perspective" piece in *The Christian Century* 108/26 (18-25 September 1991) 839-40.

fundamentalists on the right" or "the impotence and indecisiveness of moderates on the left," professors are tempted to compromise integrity in order to "hang on." It occurs to me that this is perhaps the most certain evidence of the continuity of the persistent sickness.

Do people not realize that systemic sickness and dysfunctional religious communities have no possibility of healing until those who know better take the deliberate risk of intervention? We avoid the risk because it is so enormous and because professional death is so likely. Professional death, however, may be far less painful than trying to live with a compromised integrity.

Then again, God is indeed the God both of exile *and* of resurrection.